The Renaissance of
Mark Twain's House

The Renaissance of

''Buildings and sites frequented by great men of the past often are more inspiring and evocative than their deeds or written annals.''

CICERO

Mark Twain's House

HANDBOOK FOR RESTORATION

by

WILSON H. FAUDE

With an Introduction by
OLIVER JENSEN
Senior Editor, American Heritage

Larchmont, New York

*Picture Credits: All photography from the collection
at the Mark Twain Memorial, Hartford, Connecticut.*

Book design by Alvin Schultzberg. Production supervision by
The Town House Press, Spring Valley, New York.

QUEENS HOUSE
Larchmont, New York 10538

Manufactured in the United States of America

This book is for Claire Nicoll and Janet Cole, who kept us on track and whose senses of humor and encouragement made the rough spots easier to take.

The Renaissance of Mark Twain's House

Table of Contents

Introduction by Oliver Jensen . . ix

TABLE OF CONTENTS

Introduction

There are four things every man ought to do, says Plato, before he dies: plant a tree, father a son, write a book, and build a house. If one measures Mark Twain by these standards, and winks a little at the arboreal requirement, one finds a complete man indeed. His first-born was a son, who died at two, an early intimation of the tragedies that would dog the Clemens family. Of the book production, there is scarcely need to speak here, and "the house that Mark built," the subject of this book, not only satisfied but also goes beyond anything Plato could have imagined.

That Mark's house in Hartford was as unusual in his time as the proprietor himself astonished his contemporaries. It is even more remarkable that it could be restored, after a century of troubles and changes, to its original state, so that what has been variously a boys' school, a coal warehouse, and apartments in the long interim now looks as though the owner might have just turned the key and departed an hour or so ago.

There are, to be sure, many fine examples of restoration, many of them housing great collections of art and antiques, many of them instinct with the memories of great men and events. But I know of none done more faithfully, or better documented, than the Mark Twain Memorial where, for a few brief happy years, this remarkable man wrote so many of his greatest books. The atmosphere in which a man or woman lives is infinitely more important in the case of a writer than it is in the case of others, whose lives and work are generally centered more outside the home. In the Twain House, every book, every picture, every piece of furniture, every alcove has a story to tell—and the Memorial has done a splendid job in interpreting it all and bringing it back to life.

How this came to pass, the burden of Mr. Faude's book, is as interesting to read about as the house is to visit. The guidelines or standards which he and his fellow-restorers set themselves are exact-

ing, from the research preceding every move to the careful preservation of evidence. It was an extraordinary precaution, for example, that the original but worn stenciling, once uncovered,
should not be destroyed but instead covered with canvas on which
that same design is precisely duplicated. In this spirit everything
within and without has been approached, and one can follow the
story, room by room, throughout this enormous, wandering structure. The telling of it is a fine combination of detective mystery and
affectionate biography of the talented family that inhabited the
house. The result of these painstaking labors, I would venture, is
the brightest jewel in the crown of American historical preservation.

Twain himself once remarked, "Few things are harder to put
up with than the annoyance of a good example." The achievement
of the Mark Twain Memorial is going to make things unbearable
for a lot of good people in the field of restoration.

OLIVER JENSEN

Preface

Mark Twain, America's most popular writer, is known and respected internationally. Though born and bred in Missouri, it was in Connecticut that he wrote his most popular and enduring works. While Samuel Langhorne Clemens (Mark Twain) lived in Hartford, at 351 Farmington Avenue, *The Adventures of Tom Sawyer, Adventures of Huckleberry Finn, The Prince and the Pauper, Life on the Mississippi,* and *A Connecticut Yankee in King Arthur's Court* were written. This is the story of the renaissance of that Hartford house, the rambling Victorian brick construction which was "the birthplace of some of the immortals in American literature."[1]

Today it stands as the public symbol of the man, his family, his writings and his era. Though the house had suffered as much as any of our national landmarks, today it looks as the author knew it. How was it possible to erase the wear and tear of the later occupants and uses: of the boys' school and the coal storage warehouse, of the subdivision into apartments and the modern improvements such as electricity and efficiency kitchens? Why has this restoration been singled out as "one of the finest restorations in the country, if not in the world?" What pitfalls did this restoration encounter that others would wish to avoid, and what processes were followed to solve the problems? This book presents the story of that restoration.

Presented here are the processes, the decisions and the procedures which made this restoration possible. It is hoped that other restorations will also share their secrets so that a pool of technical assistance will be available for all to use.

These master craftsmen shared our enthusiasm and our need to be accurate. Our hopes could not have been realized without their sympathetic support.

Carpentry	Norman R. Olson	
	S. Olson & Son	West Hartford, Ct.
	C.H. Dresser & Son, Inc.	Hartford, Ct.
Carving	Erwin A. Dressel	
	Dressel's Art Shop	Cheshire, Ct.
Ceramics/Tiles	Kathryn E. Narrow	Montrose, Pa.
Electrical	Fan-Craft	Avon, Ct.
	Metzger, Inc.	West Hartford, Ct.
	Selden Electric	West Hartford, Ct.
Floor coverings/Rugs	Richard D. Donchian	Hartford, Ct. &
		Hartsdale, N.Y.
Glazier	Jerry Alexander	Avon, Ct.
	Carl Lehfeldt	Glastonbury, Ct.
	Metcalfe Glass Co., Inc.	West Hardford, Ct.
Interior Decorators	Harrold De Groff	West Hartford, Ct.
	R. Curt Hasenclever	Great Barrington, Ma.
	Mrs. Samuel I. Ward,	
	The Ward Company	West Hartford, Ct.
Masonry	Ralph DePietro	South Windsor, Ct.
Metalcraft	James E. Frappe	Pittsburgh, Pa.
Painting &	Jack Forster	West Hartford, Ct.
Decorating	Walter Kryzak	East Hartford, Ct.
	Leopold Sans,	
	Sans Painting &	
	Decorating	Vernon, Ct.
	Bernhard Sans	East Hartford, Ct.
	Michael Sans	Vernon, Ct.
Photographers	Frank Beaudin,	
	Meyers Studio	Wethersfield, Ct.
	Irving Blomstrann	New Britain, Ct.
Plumbing	Eugene J. Steinberg	Bloomfield, Ct.
Roofer	Robert Ordway,	
	The C.G. Bostwick Co.	West Hartford, Ct.
Wallpaper	Samuel J. Dornsife	Williamsport, Pa.
	Mary Dunn, Nancy	
	McClelland, Inc.	New York, N.Y.
	Larsen Design Studio	New York, N.Y.
	Marburger Tapetenfabrick	
	Company	Bez Kassell, Germany

Having worked at the Mark Twain Memorial since 1963, first as a part-time summer assistant and later as Curator, the author has been privileged to see the house slowly emerge from shabbiness to its present jewel-like condition. This task involved many, many people, but the prime responsibility rested with the Restoration Committee, who served without remuneration. It was, for this writer, a valued education, a happy experience, and a great honor to serve with this dedicated group. They gave tirelessly of their time and efforts and ingenuity. Henry Darbee, Jared I. Edwards, Robert P.L. Frick, Norman Holmes Pearson, Dexter B. Peck, Mrs. Charles B. Salsbury, Robert H. Schutz, Walter K. Schwinn, Mrs. Arthur L. Shipman, Jr., Welles A. Standish II, James McA. Thomson, Joseph S. Van Why, William L. Warren.

WILSON H. FAUDE
Curator, Mark Twain Memorial

The Renaissance of Mark Twain's House

1

Guidelines and Procedures

These guidelines are those which worked in the restoration of the Mark Twain Memorial. Not every restoration is concerned with a national figure, but regardless of the specific nature of the restoration, be it a fort or a house, a room or an entire village, the philosophy behind these guidelines is valid for all restorations.

Statement of Objectives. Before any project can proceed it must be defined. A statement of objectives in general terms will serve as the overall framework for the future of the institution. Such a statement will clarify the mission of the institution and help to prevent the institution from being sidetracked, and its funds being diminished by extraneous projects.

The Board of Trustees of the Mark Twain Memorial adopted in 1955 the following statement of objectives. Periodically, they have been reviewed and modified, but the basic objectives were still in force and still viable twenty years later.

1. "To make Mark Twain's house a living memorial to him and to his family."

2. "To restore, to furnish and to present the exterior and the interior of the house as nearly as possible as they were when Mark Twain and his family occupied it, and as an example of the architecture, the decor, and the life-style of a well-to-do family living in Hartford in the 1870's."

These statements established the nature and scope of the project. It was to be a restoration, not an adaptive use project. The period of restoration was defined by the author's period of residence, that is, from 1874, when the house was built, to 1891, when the family left the house and went to Europe. By clearly defining the period a presentation so general that it lacked both focus and credibility was avoided.

Having decided what to do with the main part of the holdings, the house itself, it was important that the Trustees consider what to do with the rest of the property, including the carriage house. Item three in the Statement of Objectives stated: "To develop and maintain the exterior of the Carriage House in the style of Mark Twain's day and the interior for uses which may include an orientation center, exhibit areas, and auditorium, and other uses appropriate to the purposes of the Memorial." There would be no need for efforts to acquire carriages, tackle and other paraphernalia, thus sidetracking efforts toward the primary objective, the restoration of the house, the exteriors and the site.

Other items to be included in, or at least considered for, a Statement of Objectives are whether the organization should develop and maintain a library, a museum, foster research of the period, conduct seminars, lectures, courses of study or other similar activities. Should the institution attempt to create wide public interest in the project and in the period concerned? At the Mark Twain Memorial it was decided to develop and maintain a library and museum relating to Mark Twain, his contemporaries and his period, and to develop and foster literary and cultural research of the period.

Philosophy of Restoration. The late Professor Norman Holmes Pearson expressed the philosophy of restoration for the Mark Twain house: "A house is a document and we must only return it to the original text." It is a purist philosophy, formulated by a scholar, and it imposes severe restrictions. It also prevents important donors, however well meaning, from inflicting on the restoration furniture, paintings, or decors which do not belong. This restriction protects the credibility of the work. (If it is not a restoration, why spend all that money and effort on a figment of imagination.) Quality and accuracy are essential to a true restoration.

Research. Before any budgets, plans or wallpapers are even contemplated all that can be known to be restored must be learned. Too many restorations proceed without research, sometimes without any consideration given to original purpose of a room, or who lived there, or when. Those directing a restoration have an obligation to preserve and present our national heritage. To do this properly, much information is needed about the subject. At the Mark Twain Memorial, this meant releasing an army of volunteers to sleuth in libraries, to interview contemporaries of the Clemens children, or of later occupants. Fixing precise dates of all periods, the period of restoration and of the later ones is important for an understanding of the project. Mark Twain's daughter, Clara Clemens Samoussoud, recorded on floor plans the colors of the rooms, the placement of the furniture, the names of the rooms, anything which might document the house. A log was assembled of Mark Twain and his family's day-to-day activities, where they were on specific days, and what they did. Periodicals were found which included sketches and photographs of the interiors of this house and contemporary houses. In addition to specific information on Mark Twain's house, a great body of information was assembled on contemporary house furnishings so it could be known where Mark Twain had followed the trends, and where he had disregarded them.

Folders were then assembled, room by room, with specific headings, for the walls, ceilings, floors, window treatment, furniture, paintings, bric-a-brac, anecdotes and miscellaneous items. Each reference was fully footnoted. A binder was made with a check list of work completed and work to be done. Once this information was assembled for each room, and for each area in the room, there was one more task to be done before the restoration itself could begin.

On-site research. To return the house to its original text, it was necessary to go into the walls, the ceilings, the floors, the moldings, and the fireplaces to confirm the assembled research. The folders of information served to suggest where to look and what to expect. Of course, reporters might have taken license with descriptions, or the memories of contemporaries may have been confused. Therefore, the walls were approached with extreme care. Layer by layer, the paint was removed. Samples of each layer were preserved for study to identify the Mark Twain period. Research of the period in general, as well as this house in particular, permitted identification of those colors which were post-1891 and those which were of an earlier period. The placement of draperies, of portieres, the exact patterns of the stenciled walls and ceilings, are but a few of the clues which often survive under layers of paint. In too many restorations, these clues are not sought.

With all the research accomplished and the on-site evidence

gathered, there is still the risk of misreading the evidence or of misinterpreting the find. That is why guideline five is critical.

Preserving the evidence. All of the discoveries, notes of the discussions and the decisions which account for a restoration must be preserved. This will not only explain why a certain layer or wall treatment was accepted over another, but it will also be invaluable when years later new evidence may turn up which possibly refutes some part of the restoration and the Trustees need to know all the evidence. By preserving all the evidence, mistakes can be corrected. Photographs, measured drawings, preservation of small samples of all the layers of paint, full transcripts of the decisions, are a few of the ways in which the research can be documented.

The Committee. A restoration committee must be made up of interested persons who have special skills necessary to evaluate the information, to make the decisions and to supervise the work. At the Mark Twain Memorial the Restoration Committee was composed of Trustees, several of whom were architects, and staff, all having equal voice and vote. No decision was final which was not based on the evidence and which was not unanimous. Some decisions were delayed and delayed as opposing forces assembled new evidence to prove their interpretation of the case. If the project might have been delayed a bit, the result was more than defensible, for in every instance the decision agreed with the established evidence.

Committee meetings were held as often as necessary, but every effort was made to keep them under one hour. After an hour people begin to droop, and, when meetings have the reputation of going on forever, members tend to be late, or do not bother to show at all. If properly arranged, with members having the pertinent materials well in advance, a one hour meeting is ideal to conduct all necessary business.

Deadlines. In all projects there are deadlines, and this is particularly true of a restoration, but if the standards of the project must be compromised to meet a deadline the deadline should be changed. When a job is rushed, a compromise of quality is almost inevitable and the inferior result is seldom corrected despite good intentions. Standards are more important than deadlines. The answer to the whole question of deadlines is to plan well ahead, and to allow in that time table for Murphy's Law.*

The deadline for the opening of the Memorial was September, 1974, the Centennial of the house. Members, distinguished friends and dignitaries were coming to view the restoration. Work on one room, Susy's room, hit obstacle after obstacle. In early August it was realized that it was impossible to complete the room as it must be done. The work was stopped and the room was left in mid-passage. No one remembers that it was not completed for the opening reception but everyone benefits because the standards were observed.

Protect the Project. From the salesman who promises that his wallpaper is perfect for the restoration, from the expert who is trying to defend a theory and knows nothing about the project, from the ladies in purple hats who think they have the right to play at interior decoration, protect yourself, and more importantly, protect the project. The restoration is not for the committee who work on it, it is for future generations. It is a legacy. Restorations must be of quality. To protect the house from the compromising social, political and economic forces is to protect part of the nation's heritage.

---

*"Nothing is as simple as it seems. Everything takes longer than expected. If anything can go wrong, it will."

2

Financing the Restoration

For a restoration it is far easier to raise the necessary funds for capital improvements than it is to ask for money for operations, i.e., for staff salaries, paper towels and light bulbs. Donors know that when the capital fund drive is finished, they will not be asked to give again and again, and they can have the satisfaction of seeing that their gift was responsible for a specific change.

Appeals for restoration funds must carefully and clearly outline the project. If funds are being raised on a room by room basis, spread over a period of years, each completed task, if properly completed, will reinforce the case and instill in the minds of prospective donors the worth of the project.

At the Mark Twain Memorial, research and the lack of money dictated a room by room restoration. In some cases, as with the production of the library bookcases, the work had to be spread over several years. The basic cases were built first, then the stretcher carvings were completed and finally the corner carvings. The quality of work now presented to the visitor was beyond the resources then available. Any compromise of the standards would have been apparent immediately. With the library bookcases, as with other projects, donors appreciated the resulting quality and often gave additional amounts in order to have the job finished in one step rather than in four.

It is imperative that a restoration establish and maintain its credibility with the public. The cheap job, the rushed job, the less than quality job may save a few dollars but it places the entire project under questioning and necessitates additional expenditures later to correct the mistakes.

In the restoration of this house, two rooms were undertaken at the same time. Until one actually begins to restore a room and literally gets into the walls and the ceilings and the floors, all of the problems which are to be found there cannot be known. When two or three rooms are undertaken simultaneously, and, on-site re-search suddenly contradicts prior research, or if it appears that a whole ceiling has to be replaced, then the craftsmen can move into the next area while the Restoration Committee copes with the prob-lems.

What did this restoration cost? At the back of the book is a chart listing the major costs of this restoration. Of course, it should be remembered that the Restoration Committee members and others served on a volunteer basis, that they did most of the research, the preliminary on-site research, and even developed methods for the accomplishment of such tasks as hand-finishing a wallpaper.

Over the years the prices of certain items have increased, governmental regulations now require special equipment, or previously available items may now have to be custom made. The chart merely documents what was spent and when.

How is a restoration funded? If the Trustees of the Mark Twain Memorial in 1955 had contemplated seriously the magnitude of the task of raising the funds necessary for the restoration, they might not have endorsed the project. The Trustees voted a goal, and then they set out, step by step, as outlined in Chapter 1 to reach that goal. There were those who enthusiastically said "God will pro-vide," urging that the restoration proceed before raising the necessary funds. Others advocated a "pay as you go" procedure. Because the organization was not wealthy it was forced to adopt the "pay as you go" procedure. The lasting benefit of this was the avoidance of a deficit and the consequent discovery of ingenious methods to solve problems. Precious dollars were spent for documented, quality work. Eager to proceed, everyone went out and enlisted supporters to contribute the necessary time, energy and money.

In raising the money for the restoration, the Trustees carefully outlined the scope of each project and did not go after more money than they thought was reasonable. In many cases foundations were approached in advance of a general mailing, thus providing challenge grants. This has been a grassroots effort and most of the funds came from individuals. The fundraising mailings were carefully prepared, clearly explained the project, but did not look expensive; and in one case a mailing was underwritten by a donor. Some may assume that raising funds for the restoration of the Mark Twain Memorial, particularly in a wealthy city such as Hartford, is simple. It is no easier to raise money for Mark Twain than it is for any other project, and at times it is harder. Unfortunately, many assume that this house is well endowed, or that others will give, or that Mark Twain devotees, or his estate, or someone foots the bill.

The Trustees of the Memorial believed in the Memorial. They established a confident profile for the Memorial in the community, and as Mark Twain has increased in popularity, so has the interest in his house. It is a tribute to the Trustees, members and friends of the Mark Twain Memorial that the restoration funds were raised. They were raised because people went to work.

Separate from the restoration budget is the operational budget, the one which pays the light bills and the mundane necessities to keep the buildings open to the public. It is extremely difficult to make giving to the operational budget as attractive or exciting as giving to a restoration.

There are two basic schools of thought about balancing the operational budget. The first school holds that the endowment and the generated income (admissions, memberships, gifts and sales) must pay for the operation of the museum, and if there is a deficit it should be borne by the membership and those who visit the museum. That is, those who enjoy the museum's services should pay for that service. The second school holds that an admission fee might be charged, but if the museum were to apportion properly the expenses of its services to those who use it, the cost would be so prohibitive that only a very few would be able to enjoy the museum. This second approach acknowledges that endowment and generated income through sales and admissions will not balance the budget and, therefore, alternative funds must be provided. Both approaches address the major crisis confronting museums today, namely, being able to keep the doors open.

To date, the Mark Twain Memorial has adopted a combination of the two schools of thought. For the past several years, through very careful planning and by using highly trained volunteers, the budget has been balanced. In 1976, 81 percent of the income came from admissions and membership, seven percent from sales and lecture fees, five percent from rentals, and the remaining seven percent from endowment. Year-End Appeals have been directed to support capital expenditures. The Trustees have felt, since this is Mark Twain's house, and the organization is a public service agency, the price of admission and the individual membership must be available to everyone at a reasonable rate — that is, at a par with, or below, the national average. (One Trustee hopes that some day we will not have to charge any admission fee.)

To balance the budget, the Memorial has made a determined effort to secure additional funds, and especially to market the assets of this house, nationally and internationally. By generating articles in national and international publications, encouraging television specials, promoting slide lectures, holding benefits and membership drives, enlarging the Museum Shop, supporting community activities, and enlisting direct community participation and support, the Trustees have created a lot of interest, talk and income. One of the reasons they have been so successful is that the Trustees and the staff consciously outlined what made the Mark Twain Memorial unique and worth supporting. Instead of seeming elitist, the Memorial, as a public service agency, felt it was dependent on the public's interest, good will and financial support. So, too, there were many services which could be provided for the benefit of the community. To date, this approach has balanced the budget and, more importantly, has won many friends who, while willing to comment or to criticize, are equally willing to work for and with the Mark Twain Memorial.

Here, then, is the story of Mark Twain's house, as he knew it, as it suffered and as it stands today, looking as one visitor remarked "as if the Clemens family had just stepped out or were in the next room."

3

The Beginning 1903-1955

In 1976, as in 1881, a visitor entered the 351 Farmington Avenue house through the great front door and stepped into the hall with its marble floor, the fireplace laid with logs, and the gas lights casting quiet shadows on the red walls and silver stenciled woodwork. He might imagine the three Clemens' daughters skipping down the carpeted stairs and expect laughter to erupt from the library or dining room in response to a remark by Mark Twain. It is the Clemens' home and it is filled with their possessions and their memories.

A few years ago a visitor would not have received this impression when he crossed the threshold. So very recently it was another's house. Samuel Langhorne Clemens sold it in 1903 to the Richard M. Bissell family. Mrs. Bissell, a thoroughly modern lady, completely redecorated the house: gas lights were replaced with electric lights, wall to wall carpets were succeeded by polished hard wood floors, and the rich dark colors of Victoriana were exchanged for the grass cloth and the warm pale colors indicative of the new century. Then, from 1917 until 1922, the Bissells rented the house to Kingswood School for Boys. The house was sold in 1922 and became an unheated storage warehouse. The scurry of students was replaced by the scurry of rats. In 1927 it was sold again, and the sound of saws and hammers was heard as workmen subdivided the house into eleven apartments, each with "efficiency" kitchens and "modern" bathrooms. Absent-minded chefs and unattended baths took their toll. In 1929, under the leadership of Miss Katharine S. Day, the Friends of Hartford raised enough money to purchase the house as a Memorial to Mark Twain. The apartments on the ground floor were cleared and, to help pay off the mortgage, the Hartford Public Library established a branch library in the former Drawing Room, Dining Room, and Library. The downstairs guest room, the Mahogany Room, became the office, headquarters, and storage area for the organization. Upstairs the apartments remained, though an effort was made by Miss Day to rent only to ladies who would appreciate the building and savor the literary connection. No men or dogs were allowed.

For the next twenty-six years the tenants painted and papered according to need, or with an intent of correcting the mistaken taste of the Victorian era. Too much noise in the halls would elicit a loud "shush" from the librarian. Where Thomas Nast, Edwin Booth, William Dean Howells, Generals Sheridan and Sherman, and Sir Henry Morton Stanley had dined, strangers checked out books.

In 1951, Mrs. Arthur L. Shipman, Jr. was appointed to the Board of Trustees. She was much younger than the other members, and lived in the nearby Charles Dudley Warner house. Because she had not been through the grueling fight to save the house, Mary Shipman itched to do more with the nineteen room structure. She began to look around for contemporaries who might possess the interest, brains, and enthusiasm required to restore the house to its former elegance. Mrs. Charles B. Salsbury, Mrs. John L. Bunce, Robert H. Schutz, James McA. Thomson, Mrs. Henry R. McLane, Mrs. Dexter B. Peck, Professor Norman Holmes Pearson and others were enlisted. Skillfully, Mary Shipman encouraged the old warriors to become Honorary Trustees, thus freeing positions on the Board. With a great deal of interest and energy, the new team set to its task.

The new Board of Trustees envisioned as their goal the complete restoration of the house. They began by clearing out the "old" Memorial's offices in the former first floor guest room. What had been casually stored in cartons and in the back of closets was properly sorted, inventoried and filed. Committees were established to identify and schedule the various tasks ahead. Soon, Trustees could be found scrubbing floors or carting dirt to fill in the eroding banks, or researching the house and the period.

After a great deal of work, on April 29, 1955 the Board of Trustees voted to restore the house to the Clemens' period. The Victorian era, in 1955, was still a very unpopular period, particularly in terms of its architecture and interior decoration. The 1955 decision by the Trustees to restore the house to that period was, indeed, a farsighted one. In voting the restoration, the Board also had consciously voted several major changes in the existing operation of the

Memorial. Before too long it would be necessary to evict the Mark Twain Branch of the Hartford Public Library, the main source of income for the house. Eventually all of the ladies who occupied apartments in the house also would have to be evicted. Conservative Trustees were desperately worried that the visionary plans for the restoration would not only result in the loss of any real income, but would also place the entire structure in jeopardy.

Committees went to work to offset the future loss of income. The general public was invited to become members of the Memorial and events were held to encourage community interest. Speakers were enlisted, including the Governor of Connecticut, the Honorable John Davis Lodge, who gave readings from Mark Twain. The Newsletter was created to inform members of past and future events. The annual Frog Jump, presided over by the Mayor of Hartford, was inaugurated by the Memorial and the Children's Museum of Hartford.

The membership grew from some one hundred members to over five hundred in a few short years, and has been growing ever since. By not depending solely on one or two individuals for money, and by expanding determined efforts to encourage community support for the preservation and restoration of the house, the Trustees established wide and continuing support for the Memorial.

In 1958 the Hartford Public Library vacated the ground floor of the house, leaving the Trustees with great empty spaces, some day to be restored but which needed at the moment a fresh coat of paint. Research had provided reference to the colors of the rooms, and the rooms were painted to correspond generally with those colors. To furnish the rooms and to provide some semblance of the period, the Trustees raided their own and friends houses of everything which seemed appropriate. These furnishings gave the rooms an identity and sparked greater community interest in the project.

The restoration, from its inception to its completion in 1974, took over twenty years. To many, that will seem like a very extended period. In light of the accomplishments, it was obviously a worthwhile effort. The house again looks as if the author and his family still lived here. It was a result that began with extensive research.

4

Some Notes on the Owner

Mark Twain was born Samuel Langhorne Clemens on November 30, 1835 in the small town of Florida, Missouri. At the age of four his family moved to Hannibal, on the banks of the mighty Mississippi. In 1853 Sam Clemens became a printer's apprentice to his brother, Orion, in Keokuk, Iowa. Later he served as a river pilot, as a soldier (for two weeks), as a miner, and as a newspaperman. He first used the pen name Mark Twain in the newspaper *Territorial Enterprise,* in Virginia City, Nevada, in 1862. In 1866 he joined the *Morning Call* in San Francisco and, as a newspaperman, visited the Sandwich Islands (Hawaii) and wrote travel letters for several California papers. In 1867, "The Celebrated Jumping Frog of Calaveras County" was published and that same year Sam Clemens joined an excursion to the Mediterranean and the Holy Land. On that journey he met Charles Jervis Langdon whose sister he was later to marry. Clemens sent to his editor in San Francisco a series of columns describing the sights and sounds of Europe and the East. These columns achieved national syndication, and, on his return, Clemens received an invitation from Elisha Bliss of the American Publishing Company in Hartford, Connecticut, to explore the possibility of turning that series of letters into a book. So, in 1868, Samuel Clemens came to Hartford.

When he first visited Hartford, Clemens was impressed by the city and especially by its homes which he described as "massive private hotels." Each house, he wrote to his readers in San Francisco, was "buried from sight in parks and forests of these noble trees." He found the city a "vision of refreshing green," concluding, "You do not know what beauty is if you have not been here."[1] On the edge of Hartford was a literary colony, Nook Farm, an unfenced enclave, where lived Harriet Beecher Stowe, Charles Dudley Warner, Francis Gillette, and Isabella Beecher Hooker.

On February 2, 1870, Samuel Clemens and Olivia Langdon

Samuel L. Clemens, at the age of 35, wearing his great sealskin coat.

Olivia Langdon at the time of her marriage to Samuel L. Clemens.

were married in Elmira, New York, and moved to Buffalo where he was an editor of the *Buffalo Express*. The Buffalo period was filled with gloom and loneliness. Olivia's father died, Livy's best friend died, and their first born, a son (Langdon Clemens) was born prematurely.

In 1871 the Clemenses moved from Buffalo to Hartford and rented the home of John and Isabella Hooker, in Nook Farm. Hartford stood at the green end of the road from Hannibal. It was everything Buffalo was not. Nook Farm represented prestige and friends. It was a refreshing and badly needed haven.

Though among friends, the Clemenses soon chafed at living in

Edward T. Potter, the architect for Mark Twain's house.

another's house. The house had been designed for Isabella Beecher Hooker, and Mrs. Clemens had commented, "You'd know it was built by a Beecher: it's so queer."[2] In 1873 the Clemenses decided to build their own house in Hartford, to settle down and establish roots.

At the suggestion of their neighbors, the George Warners, they commissioned Edward Tuckerman Potter of New York as the architect. The selected lot was in Nook Farm, bordered on the east by Mrs. Stowe's home, on the south by the Warner's, on the west by the Park River and on the north by Farmington Avenue.

It was a marvelous house and was close enough to completion by the fall of 1874 for the Clemens family to move in. A local newspaper commented that it was one "of the oddest looking buildings in the state ever designed for a dwelling, if not in the whole country." William Dean Howells knew better. He sensitively appreciated that "Clemens was building the stately mansion in which he satisfied his love of magnificence as if it had been another sealskin coat."[3]

Langdon, the Clemens' first born, had died at the age of two in 1872. That same year Olivia Susan Clemens was born, followed in 1874 by Clara, and in 1880 by Jean. Of the three daughters, Susy was the favorite and her life closely parallels the life and happenings in the Hartford house. It was Susy who began a biography of her father when she was 13, who wrote musicals and plays for the family to perform, and on whom her parents and sisters showered attention.

In 1891, unfortunate financial investments (the failure of the Paige Compositor, and of the Charles L. Webster Publishing Company) placed a great strain on the Clemens family. They were forced to close the Hartford house and move to Europe where the cost of living was appreciably less. For five years Mark Twain wrote, traveled, lectured and wrote. Finally, in 1896, the bills were paid, there was money in the bank, and they could be a family again. Susy and Jean were in America, in Hartford, staying with the Charles Dudley Warners. Katy Leary, the family's faithful maid, was also in Hartford, living on Spring Street. Word came for Susy, Jean and Katy to join the rest of the family in England. All was packed and made ready. On the day they were to leave Hartford,

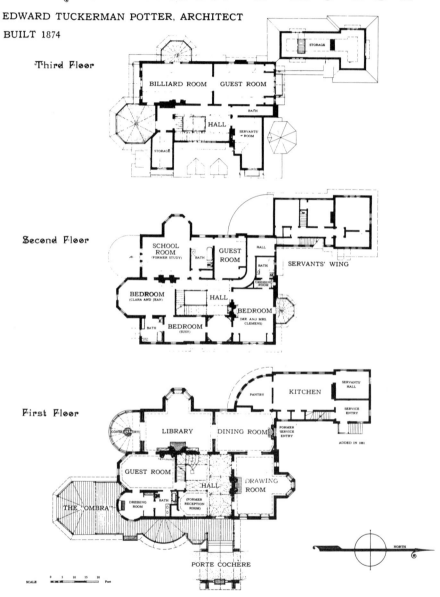

The floor plan of the Hartford house. Clemens estimated that it cost $131,000 for the land, the house and the furnishings in 1874.

Mark Twain's house as seen from Farmington Avenue.

In 1955 the south facade was dominated by a great firescape.

The south facade restored to its original lines.

The east facade after a January snow and ice storm.

The east facade in the late spring.

The front hall in 1958 served as guides center and sales area.

The front hall restored.

The original Tiffany decorations discovered beneath layers of paint.

Susy became ill— spinal meningitis. The Hartford house was reopened and Susy was settled in the Mahogany Guest Suite on the first floor. On August 18th, Livy's brother sent a cablegram to Mark Twain: "Susy could not stand brain congestion and meningitis and was peacefully released today."[4]

The Hartford period was over. Livy would never enter the house again. To Mark Twain it had become a shrine, a hallowed place. But it was not possible to live there. For seven years they left the house as it had been, and finally sold it in 1903.

There was something remarkable about the house and the Hartford period. During this period Mark Twain wrote *The Adventures of Tom Sawyer, Adventures of Huckleberry Finn, A Connecticut Yankee in King Arthur's Court, A Tramp Abroad, The Prince and the Pauper* and *Life on the Mississippi.* Later, after Susy's death, after the Hartford period, the author's bitterness and pessimism grew. He was not an intellectual philosopher of gloom — rather a family man for whom life had grown sour. Because the Hartford period was so sweet, twilight was all the more bitter. In retrospect, the Hartford house was the only home the family ever knew.

The Clemens family on the porch of the Hartford house in 1885. Left to right: Clara, Livy, Jean, Sam and Susy. The dog's name was Hash.

5

In Pursuit of the Decorators

In the 1950's the decorations of the Victorian era, and especially the art glass of Mr. Louis Comfort Tiffany, were considered to be "unfortunate." The period was thought of as a distant nightmare of dark rooms and ostentatious plunder, the Tiffany's work was considered a mirror of a decadent time. Would anyone consider, seriously consider, restoring the house to *that* period? The house and the accumulated evidence answered the question. Early research confirmed that in 1881 Mark Twain had hired Louis Comfort Tiffany and his firm of Associated Artists to redecorate the Hartford house. It was during the 1880's that the three Clemens children were raised, when the major writings were completed, and it was the most documentable period. Also, from a visitor's point of view, the rich 1880's decorations would represent the mature taste of the Clemenses.

It was necessary then to research the work of Associated Artists, as they were an important factor in the complex series of elements which had finally shaped this house into a home for the Clemens family and which must be reconstructed if the evidence were to be properly interpreted.

Until recently, all that was generally known about Mr. Tiffany and Associated Artists was that they were a New York professional decorating firm which had worked on a number of buildings and homes, including the White House in 1882. Of the firm's principals only Mrs. Candace Thurber Wheeler wrote extensively, producing articles and books. In her writing she presented clear, concise concepts for room decoration, for materials and design. It was essential to locate her letters or journals as they might verify and further enunciate those concepts, and perhaps specifically document the 1881 decoration of the Clemens house.

Mrs. Wheeler once had a summer house in Onteora, New York, which she and her brother, Francis B. Thurber, had built.

The New York Social Register listed a Mrs. Francis B. Thurber III, and on the chance that she was the right family and, perhaps, even owned the summer home, she was contacted. Mrs. Thurber cheerfully responded, and three weeks later the author went to "Pennyroyal," Candace Wheeler's summer home.

Summer homes are curious things and usually they have been completely stripped after each owner, or they have remained as an accumulation of all the owners. "Pennyroyal" was an accumulation, from Mrs. Wheeler onward. The result of that first visit to "Pennyroyal" was that the Memorial's collection was enriched by some 80 fabrics designed by Mrs. Wheeler. More importantly, Mrs. Thurber provided names of other relatives who generously contributed letters, notes and anecdotes. This research on Mrs. Wheeler, when joined with similar studies of Tiffany, deForest and Colman, created a clear picture of the decorating firm.

Associated Artists was created in 1879 by the partnership of Tiffany, Colman, deForest and Mrs. Wheeler. In the four years of their partnership, the firm captured many of the most prestigious commissions of the day, including the decoration of the Seventh Regiment Armory, the White House, the Madison Square Theater, and the homes of Samuel Clemens, the Kemps, and the Vanderbilts. Each commission was approached with a freshness and an ingenuity that Cecelia Waern, an English visitor in the 1890's, likened to "a clever milliner adapting adroitly to any problem presented."[1]

Louis Comfort Tiffany (1848-1933), the son of Charles Lewis Tiffany, founder of the New York jewelry firm, Tiffany and Company, began his career as a painter, studying under George Inness and Samuel Colman. He traveled abroad with Colman, particularly in North Africa and Europe, and in 1877, with John LaFarge, founded the Society of American Artists. Although Tiffany is primarily remembered for his designs in irridescent and stained glass, he exhibited a number of paintings at the Centennial Exposition in Philadelphia in 1876. He was an exponent of the belief that a credible artist should not confine himself to a single medium.

Samuel Colman (1832-1920) studied under Asher B. Durand from 1860 to 1862, and, from 1871 to 1876, he traveled in Europe and North Africa. He assembled an important collection of Japanese prints and fabrics, some of which were the impetus for many of his design motifs. A founder and first president of the American Watercolor Society, he was well known not only for his paintings, but also for his designs in fabrics, wall papers and ceiling papers.

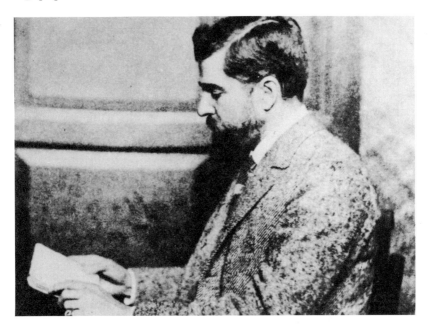

Louis C. Tiffany about the time he formed Associated Artists.

Lockwood deForest (1850-1920) like Tiffany and Colman, began his career as a painter, studying with Herman Corrode in Rome, and with Frederic Church and James M. Hart. From 1875 until 1878 he traveled in Europe, Egypt, Syria and India. In 1881 he re-established workshops in Ahmadabad, India, employing from forty to one hundred men and boys for the revival of Indian designs in wood and brass. He is best known for his introduction of these materials into the design schemes of fashionable homes, such as those of Mr. Hamilton Fish, Mr. Andrew Carnegie, and Mrs. Potter Palmer.

Candace Thurber Wheeler (1828-1923) was neither an artist nor a professional designer, but a housewife in Hollis, Long Island,

*Candace Wheeler was a partner in Associated Artists and then in
1883 managed the firm on her own.*

until she visited the Centennial Exposition of 1876. There she saw
the English exposition of art needlework from the Kensington
School, a school established to aid economically deprived
gentlewomen. Realizing that such a society could provide work for
thousands of hapless women, Mrs. Wheeler established in New
York, in 1877, the Society of Decorative Art. Prominent artists, including Tiffany, deForest, Colman and LaFarge were enlisted to
teach classes in design. Mrs. Wheeler's concern for the art educa-

tion of women led her to write many books on home decoration, including: *The Development of Embroidery in America, How to Make Rugs, Principles of Home Decoration*, and her autobiography, *Yesterdays in a Busy Life*. By 1879 Mrs. Wheeler was well known as a designer of fine fabrics and embroideries. She had won several competitions, and art journals had featured her designs. That same year Tiffany came to Mrs. Wheeler, inviting her to join Colman, deForest and himself in a business concerned with interior design and decoration.

The work of this partnership must be seen against the backdrop of the period. In the 1870's a genuinely modern style in the decorative arts emerged in England quite separate from the heavily patterned lambrequined designs usually associated with that decade. The aesthetic movement, as this ubiquitous style was labeled, was led in England by E.W. Godwin, James A. McN. Whistler and Christopher Dresser. The American counterpart to the aesthetic movement was manifested in the work of Louis C. Tiffany and Associated Artists. They saw themselves as the arbiters of good taste, and consequently retained a tight control over their projects. The greatest factor which brought Associated Artists recognition and prestigious commissions was their notion of beauty, to which they consistently and successfully appealed. "The first principle of beauty is appropriateness," Mrs. Wheeler wrote, "and no room could be beautiful which failed to express the individuality of the occupant."[2]

For the Clemenses, Associated Artists redecorated the front hall, drawing room, dining room, library, downstairs guest room, and the second and third floor halls. The original contract spelled out between Samuel Clemens and Associated Artists survives among the Mark Twain Papers in Berkeley, but it only vaguely outlines the work to be done, e.g., "walls papered or painted at our option."[3] The research into the firm and the details of their other commissions and the evidence revealed in on-site investigations, made it possible to proceed with the restoration. The decision to stick to the evidence and to restore the house to the Tiffany period turned out to be extremely fortunate. In 1977, the Memorial was the only surviving commission by Associated Artists which was open to the public.

6

The Exterior

In the January, 1877, issue of the *Travelers Record,* Mark Twain described his Hartford home:

This is the house that Mark Built.
These are the bricks of various hue
And shape and position, straight and askew,
With the nooks and angles and gables too,
Which make up the house presented to view,
The curious house that Mark built.[1]

Others have been more critical, describing the design as "God awful." Over the years, and due to various "improvements," the house had lost a great deal of its charm and its original lines had been obscured. Many of the bricks were painted white. A fire escape jutted from the third story to accommodate the apartment tenants. The wood trim was painted a deep, and not very attractive, blue-black. It was hard to appreciate the influence which German buildings or Violet LeDuc had had on architect Edward Tuckerman Potter. In fact, it was even hard to appreciate the building as anything but the home of Mark Twain.

The building had many exterior problems and the *Boston Daily Globe* headlined the most important one when, in January, 1960, in an article on the house, declared, "It could stand a new roof." Patched, caulked, and repaired over the years, the slates, the flashing and the tar had deteriorated badly. Inclement weather revealed many leaks. Having just paid off the mortgage of $100,000, the Trustees and members of the Memorial were not especially eager to try to raise the required $25,000. Yet the roof was beyond repair, and so, in September, 1959, letters went out asking for support. Before any work could begin on the roof, Trustee James Thomson and others scaled the peaks and gables, photographing, measuring and recording every detail. Despite the severe patching and the haphazard repairs, many of the original

Mark Twain's house as it looked from 1881–1903.

The south facade of the Hartford house. This stereopticon view
taken in 1875 is from a set belonging to Sam Clemens.

slates survived in their original three-color pattern. From these, the
pattern for the whole roof could be accurately reconstructed —
where the design began, where it changed, where it ended. All of
the original slates were carefully removed and samples were sent to
Vermont, where the colors were matched. New underlayers and
new flashings were installed, and finally, with photographs and
measurements in hand, workmen duplicated the color patterns.
The original slates were reused where possible. The striking im-
provement achieved by the restored roof impelled the restoration of
the rest of the exterior to its original state.

In 1960, many of the exterior bricks had been painted, creating stripes of black and white. Literary references contradicted this exterior and sparked investigation of the actual surface. In checking layer by layer, it was discovered that the black color was consistent for all the layers, but beneath the first layer of the white paint was a strong vermilion color. Vermilion and black stripes? Vermilion and black stripes with a deep red trim and a three-colored, diamond patterned roof? Research, period letters and comments verified the unusual combination. These were the "bricks of various hue" and thus they had to be restored.

At this time the great unsightly fire escape was removed from the south facade. To comply with the fire codes, a second interior stair to the third floor was discreetly installed where two bathrooms had been. While it is desirable to sacrifice nothing, the exchange of two bathrooms for the restoration of an entire facade seemed a reasonable choice. The roof was completed in June, 1961, and the restoration of the wood trim and the bricks was completed in the fall of 1962. What was the public reaction? Quite literally — it was a smashing success! There were several bad accidents on Farmington Avenue caused by drivers who became hypnotized by the fantastic painted brick courses.

With every house, particularly a national landmark, one must schedule monthly and yearly maintenance — checking for termites, checking the gutters, slates, and flashing. The cost of repainting a Victorian house can be formidable. Because of a limited budget, every year the Memorial checks and paints a part of the house, thus spreading out the work and the financial strain. By constant checking and maintenance, the exterior is kept in sound condition. Beginning in 1975, a specified area of the exterior woodwork was completely scraped of its one hundred years of paint, unsound wood replaced, and then painted. In this manner the condition of the wood was checked and the fine, crisp original lines retrieved.

With deep red trim, its vermilion and black striped courses, its patterned roof, the Mark Twain House appeared in 1977 as in 1874.

The east facade of the house as it looks today.

7

Front Hall

Perhaps the most important public room in any Victorian house was its great front hall. It created the first impression, the feeling for the house, and the affluence of the owners. From it a visitor might be ushered into the more private regions of a house, or be asked to wait politely in one of the great chairs which occupied this space. To one side there was usually a small reception room where the lady of the house might conduct business with a tradesman or a book seller, discreetly out of the family areas and the main stream of daily traffic.

On the left of the Clemens' hall, in 1874, was a small reception room, and off the main hall were the doors for the drawing room, dining room and library. The far left-hand corner was dominated by the staircase and its carved newel post. From this point there was an open vista up to the third floor. In 1880, the Clemenses changed the scale of the hall by eliminating the reception room, thus creating a large open space which Will Clemens, Mark Twain's nephew, described as "an immense square hall, the floor of which is in marble tiles of peculiar pattern. A winding staircase, very wide and massive, of heavy carved English oak extends about."[1]

On festive occasions the hall fireplace would be ablaze, particularly at Christmas or Thanksgiving, or when Susy celebrated her third birthday in the hall. In one corner stood a bust of Mark Twain by Karl Gerhardt, in another the music box, and everywhere "easy chairs, rugs, cushions, and carved furniture that instantly invite the guest to lounge."[2]

The fireplace in the front hall was constructed with the flue to the right, thus affording space directly over the fireplace for a window looking into the drawing room. In 1881, Tiffany installed in this opening an interior stained glass window. The window represented "a young girl symbolizing autumn with fruit and flowers around her."[3] To date, this window has not been found.

Mrs. Clemens was willing to sell the Tiffany windows with the house, but she was not willing to give them away. Was the window, along with the other Tiffany windows, sold? Was it sent on commission to an art store, or smashed? Some day the answer, or the window, may be found.

In 1903 all of the Clemens' furniture was removed from the house, and by 1957 the hall had become a sales area, complete with tables laden with books for sale. Runners, postcard racks, knick knacks, and the usual plethora of gift shop items greeted the guest. The hall resembled the downstairs of an old hotel, as visitors mingled, and bought cards and souvenirs. It had seen better days. Occasionally, one of the tenants would bustle by, laden with groceries, and ascend the stairs to the private regions above. It was the perfect setting for a murder mystery, and in fact Lee Thayer, author of over fifty "crimes," who was a summer resident in 1945, wrote *Murder Stalks the Circle*, using the house and neighborhood as the locale.

In 1963 the Restoration Committee began preliminary on-site investigation of the walls and ceiling of the front hall. At that time the Committee established a standard procedure for all areas house. First check all letters, photographs, and other documents, and, secondly, undertake careful, meticulous scraping of all wall and ceiling areas to establish the sequence of all paint, papering, colors and designs.

To investigate the various layers of paint on the walls, the master painter used a combination of solvents, benzol, toluol, acetone, methyl alcohol, lacquer thinner and menthol. Time and the willingness to proceed very slowly were prime considerations. By this procedure, in some rooms old wallpapers were found sealed beneath the layers of paint, documentation which would have been lost if the master craftsman had not proceeded as carefully as he did.

When all evidence was located, the walls and ceilings were sealed with a clear acrylic coating to protect the remains of the original. All of the designs were traced, photographed, and colors matched. Then a walltex canvas was applied to the walls and ceilings and where stencil designs were found, these were exactly reproduced on the canvas. Where wallpaper was found (and sometimes this was found only by removing a fireplace mantel, a

Lydia Emmet of Associated Artists drew this sketch for a domestic window titled "Autumn." It is possible that this is the window which dominated the front hall.

door frame or wood trim) sometimes the evidence survived in the form of rolled-up fragments caught on top of a molding where they had remained after being scraped off the wall by a putty knife. Further investigation was required to locate existing papers or to have a new paper reproduced from such discovery. At the same time the walls were examined, original locations for gas fixtures appeared. These places were provided with electrical wiring snaked through the walls so that eventually, with minimum disruption, original or period fixtures could be installed.

"Improvements" to the house over the years made it impossible merely to clean the walls down to the original state. This was a methodical deductive process, first studying all the existing evidence and then proceeding with the work of restoring each element to its original state.

There is always a debate about what to do with the evidence which has been uncovered, particularly when that evidence consists of painted decorations on a wall which is to be restored. In some restorations the evidence is merely recorded in notebooks, and then the walls are repainted to match the original decorations. In others, the decorations are removed, but this is a risky procedure at best, which records the pattern but does not necessarily record the exact placement of those patterns. It preserves merely a fragment of the text. Because the members of the Restoration Committee were all amateurs, and because of the philosophy behind this restoration, and most certainly because the Restoration Committee and the Board of Trustees did not think of themselves as infallible, and as two or more years might elapse between the discovery and having enough funds to restore that area, a great effort was made to save every piece of evidence located in the on-site investigation.

How was this possible?

When establishing the decorative sequence, layer by layer, the sequence was preserved on film, in drawings, and, unobtrusively, behind a door. By coating the documented surface with the non-yellowing acrylic and then covering it with a walltex canvas on which the designs could be reproduced, it was possible to preserve the document. In some areas pristine fragments were protected under glass, not covered with acrylic or canvas, thus providing an extra check, and a feature interesting to visitors. Only when a crumbling ceiling or wall needed to be removed were the elements cut out and preserved. In all cases the rooms were extensively photographed and measured, and, when fragments had to be removed, they were specifically keyed to the drawings and stored for future use.

A common mistake in most restorations is to rush the project, or to ignore the fact that most Victorian homes were painted with a calcimine base paint which easily washes off. Stenciled decorations were often made with more durable milk and dry products. A wall or any surface must be treated with the same care and technical skill used to restore a painting. Once the mistake has been made, the job hurried, and the evidence lost, that documentation cannot be recovered. In a preservation effort, all the evidence must be preserved, for future reference as well as to have the necessary facts on hand for the immediate restoration. Memory is highly unreliable and must not be solely relied upon. All facts must be preserved to avoid well-intentioned but inaccurate interpretation. The detailed record of the evidence also helps to suppress one's personal taste and avoids applying contemporary aesthetic values to the restoration of a past period.

Beneath the cream yellow walls, beneath layer after layer, there appeared, suddenly and unexpectedly, a dark venetian red, covered with geometric patterns in black, and, on the ceiling, similar designs were uncovered, complemented with an overall silver design. The designs matched the faded designs on the woodwork which had been attributed to Tiffany and his firm. Further checking revealed that beneath the red was a coat of grey, a primer coat, and then plaster. This was appropriate as Tiffany had not decorated the house, he had redecorated it, and earlier Mrs. Clemens had complained of the pale grey walls. Research documented the firm's preference for red as the most appropriate color for a hall. Candace Wheeler had written the Pompeian and Damascus reds were particularly desirable, as they had enough yellow in their composition to harmonize with the yellows of oiled wood. On the confident assumption that the "Tiffany layer" had indeed been located, all the modern coats of paint were carefully removed so the entire decorative scheme was exposed and could be photographed, traced and measured.

*Using the same techniques which Tiffany had, the mastercraftsman
Leo Sans hand stencils the ceiling of the front hall.*

It was vital to know exactly what the decorator had done and if
and where he had altered the pattern, the scheme, the design. On
the landing, between the first and second floors, the red abruptly
changed to olive green, with a different stencil design in gold.

When the hall was enlarged in 1880 by the removal of the
reception room, the new space was unbalanced since the ceiling of

the former reception room lacked the elaborate formal star- patterned wooden beams of the hall. Tiffany unified the space by
reproducing in stencils the beam pattern, and then completed the
scheme with an overall ceiling design.

In 1966, when the hall's wall and ceiling designs were reproduced, one of the workmen carefully began removing some of the
grimy dirt on the woodwork. Suddenly the original yellowed (always
assumed gold) stenciled pattern on the woodwork emerged as silver.
Was the effect originally silver or gold? The question was settled by
this description of the hall: "The doors and woodwork are of pol-

*Between the first and second floor halls the designs and the colors
abruptly changed from red and black and silver below to
olive green and gold above.*

ished wood, covered with stencil designs in metallic paint, so that at a short distance they look as if inlaid with mother-of-pearl."[4]

Unfortunately, many of the silver designs had been worn away. Should the worn designs merely be replaced, thus creating an uneven effect, or should they be recorded, traced and photographed, and completely reproduced? Should the excess varnish be removed, leaving the designs incomplete but intact?

Louis C. Tiffany never actually stenciled these walls but just supervised the work. In 1881 these designs were meant to brighten and lighten the space.

The Restoration Committee, after a considerable debate, decided to clean the panels and reproduce the designs exactly so they would look as they had during the Clemens period. One panel was left completely untouched for future reference.

In 1968 when the Visitors' Center was opened in the Carriage House belonging to the Stowe-Day Foundation, all of the books, the guides and the prattle were removed from the hall to this new and more efficient space. The money changers were removed from the temple. In their place were returned the comfortable chairs, the little rugs, and a chandelier with etched glass globes.

From the attic of the New Britain Art League came the original circular seat, all tufted and surmounted with an "artichoke." The Stowe-Day Foundation loaned the bust of Henry Ward Beecher that had belonged to the Clemenses, and from the neighboring Perkins house came a period music box. The Langdon family gave the original bust of Clemens by Gerhardt, which originally stood in the hall. Members and friends donated period furnishings to fill out the corners, to complete the scene.

In 1977, when the great front door swung open and a visitor entered the hall, he saw a unified room, delicious and charming. The light striking the marble floor and bouncing off the woodwork with its silver stenciling was softly reflected in the ceiling. Once again it looked as it did in the Clemens period, warm and inviting, and what more could be asked?

The front hall restored.

8

Drawing Room

In the fall of 1966, following the restoration of the front hall, the restoration of the Drawing Room began. An 1889 photograph survived of the Clemens girls performing Susy's play, "A Love Chase," in the drawing room, showing what the wall decorations had been. Behind the girls, in the photograph, were designs of grapes and bellflowers and zigzag borders, apparently in a reflective material, as well as part of a statue, presumably Mercury, which once had been in the house. In 1959, in an interview with Mrs. Herbert A. Taylor, who as a child had played in the house, it was learned that "Mrs. Candace Wheeler of the 'Associated Artists' in New York and my aunt, Mrs. Edward Jenkins of New Haven, worked out the new color scheme of that room which had been awful Victorian rosebud carpet and blue satin curtains before, a 'wedding present gift,' from Mrs. Clemens' parents."[1]

The drawing room of a Victorian house was usually formal in setting and atmosphere. Associated Artists felt that it was important to retain this atmosphere of "delicacy and elegance" and Mrs. Wheeler recommended that "the wall . . . be hung with paper . . . or decorated with a scattered design in gold or silver." The color might be "blue or green or rose and cream," but the strongest consideration was that "the end result be delicate."[2]

As carefully as before, layer after layer of paint was removed until at last the designs so visible in the 1889 photograph, silver grapes and bellflowers on a salmon pink ground, and, beneath the chair rail, silver paisley designs were uncovered. They were far more brilliant and lively than expected. The walls were carefully cleaned down to the Tiffany decorations. The ceiling was another matter. Under only a few layers of paint, long before the level of the Tiffany layer, there was just plaster. Someone had replaced the ceiling and all evidence of the original decorations had been lost, ex-

In 1889 the Clemens girls and friends performed "A Love Chase" in the Drawing Room. The cast included Clara as 'Art,' Daisy Warner as 'Literature,' Jean as 'Cupid,' Susy, and Fanny Freese as 'The Shepherd Boy.'

cept that there was a gas pipe in the center indicating a central gas chandelier. It was decided in 1967 to restore only the walls and woodwork and for the moment merely to paint the ceiling the same color as the walls.

Behind where the original pier glass mirror had been reinstalled there was no stenciling. The mirror was returned to the house in 1959 by Mr. Thomas Mellander of the Y&M Upholstery Company, 239 Farmington Avenue. Mr. Mellander had acquired the mirror from Mrs. William Trapp, who had purchased it at the 1903 auction of Mark Twain's house. When the Memorial received this mirror, it was covered with painted bands of gold, silver, rose and cream, and was heavily covered with dirt. Here and there beneath the paint, there was visible the rosewood, ebonized wood, mahogany, highlighted with gold. A sketch of the mirror, indicating its 1959 condition and the placement of the painted bands, was made. Then the mirror went to C.H. Dresser & Son, Inc. to be

The Drawing Room when it served as a reading room for the public library.

restored. It was a high style mirror of the 1870's, complete with a porcelain plaque. All of the brightness and elegance had been covered by the paint. When the mirror was returned to the house, cleaned and restored, it was placed against the east wall in the only space it would fit. When the wall was being scraped to uncover the Tiffany layer, it was gratifying to discover that Tiffany's artisans had not removed the mirror in redecorating the room, thus accounting for that lack of stenciling behind it. That undecorated space established the exact height and placement of the mirror.

During the restoration of this room in 1966, a letter from Mrs. Clemens to Mr. Franklin G. Whitmore came to light, stating that the mirror "was originally fitted into the Buffalo house and was brought from there to Hartford. It was kept always rosewood and gilt until we decorated the drawing room then we painted the frame to match the window casings."[3] Preserved in the files was the sketch of the mirror as it had been, with its painted bands of rose and gold and silver. If that evidence had not been recorded and preserved, the documentation on the mirror would have been lost. To the horror of some, the rose and the cream, the gold and the silver bands were then reduplicated. Instead of dominating the scheme, the mirror now reflected it, carrying the space but not dominating it.

In scraping the window casings for the restoration, it was revealed that, though the window frames were built for interior shutters, no screw holes or marks could be found to indicate that shutters ever had been installed. The marks of the drapery rods survived but no shutter marks. It was voted not to install shutters until some evidence appeared to dictate them.

Contemporaries noted that the velvet draperies were of a soft blue, and, after studying all commercially available fabrics, a soft cut blue velvet was selected which resembled the pattern in an original photograph and harmonized with the walls. The 1889 photograph gave indication of elaborate panels of embroidery on the draperies and portieres below the chair rail, probably the work of Mrs. Wheeler and her department of Associated Artists. Lacking any samples or a positive knowledge of exactly the colors and handling of such designs, the Restoration Committee elected not to try to recreate the embroidered panels, but merely to indicate the banding, their placement, thus preserving the scale, but not at-

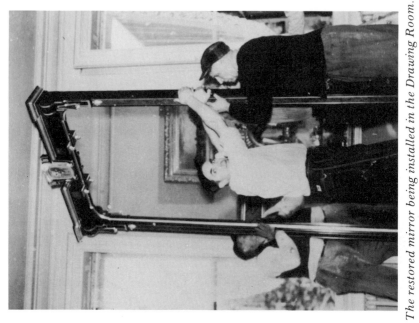

The restored mirror being installed in the Drawing Room.

The original Drawing Room mirror was located in an upholstery shop.

tempting anything more. Because Associated Artists had discarded lace curtains for sheer Indian muslin or tambour, a similarly suitable fabric was installed.

The original chandelier was returned from the Wadsworth Atheneum where Mrs. Bissell had deposited it. Gerhardt's plaster statue of Mercury had been given by the Clemenses to Mark Twain's business manager, Franklin G. Whitmore. In 1964 Mercury was located in the loft of the Whitmore carriage house, where he had sat quietly those many years. Shells in gilt cases, statues, water colors in gilt frames, were acquired to correspond with the notes of Clara Clemens and others. Once again, as Clara Clemens remembered, the room "presented an impression of hospitable light — or a suggestively divine quality."[4]

There was still one element which was out of tune, detracting from the tone of the atmosphere, and that was the ceiling. In 1967 the ceiling was painted pink, but by 1974 its plainness, its inability to carry the light, was apparent. In 1879 Warren Fuller and Company had produced a promotional booklet, "What Should We Do with Our Walls?" which featured wallpapers by Louis C. Tiffany and Samuel Colman. In it Clarence Cook urged "white ceilings are, or ought to be, disagreeable to everybody."[5] He recommended the work of Tiffany and Colman. All known photographs of similar rooms decorated by the Associated Artists were studied. In 1974 a simple formal rosette was installed around the base of the chandelier and the walls' stenciled border designs were adapted to the perimeter of the ceiling. The result is appropriate. It carries the light and the tone, but does not dominate the scheme.

The Drawing Room provides a rich, delicate atmosphere. One can imagine the formal teas which were held here, see the girls at their dancing lessons, the meetings of the Saturday Morning Club and the Browning Society, or the evenings when Samuel Clemens presided at the grand piano, singing Negro spirituals and, with Susy beside him, playing Beethoven or Chopin. Because of the refinement and order of this space, one can also appreciate that, after being up most of the night preparing Christmas for their children, it was to this room that Sam and Livy Clemens retreated for a quiet breakfast and savored the peace in which they opened their own presents.

9

Dining Room

Dinner parties in the Clemens house were frequent, brilliant affairs. Albert Bigelow Paine, Mark Twain's biographer, described the scene: "The best minds, the brightest wits gathered around Mark Twain's table. Booth, Barrett, Sheridan, Sherman, Howells, Aldrich! They all assembled and many more. There was always someone on the way to Boston or New York who addressed himself for the day or night, or for a brief call, to the Mark Twain fireside."[1] The Clemenses were whole-souled hosts, and their daughters recalled sitting on the landing, listening for the laughter to pour from the room. Their father had told another funny tale.

Those days were over in 1891, and the room of so many late, late evenings where the sherry, claret and champagne, and the beef or duck, and the ice creeeam in the shape of flowers or of cherubs mingled happily, were gone. In 1929 the room was the check-out desk for the library, its white walls and impersonal furniture illuminated by small electric sconces or the cold, even, north light from a window which was directly over the fireplace. The window's placement was possible by placing the flue on the right, and Mark Twain liked the window for it allowed him "to see the snowflakes fall to meet the rising flames."[2] How had the Clemens family known this space which was now so cold and formidable?

For a dining room, according to Mrs. Wheeler of the Associated Artists, if the room "has a cold northern exposure, reds, golds, or browns are indicated."[3] The dining room of the Clemens' house, with its principal window directly over the fireplace on the north wall, provided the Restoration Committee with at least a tentative guideline to follow in restoring that room.

In 1962 Board member Mary Shipman went to the Cooper-Hewitt Museum of Decorative Arts & Design, New York City, to research their extensive wallpaper collection for possible clues and

advice on period papers which might be used in the restoration.
Mrs. Hedy Backlin of that Museum produced a sample of a gilt and
embossed machine-printed paper which, though very dark and dirty, resembled imitation leather. The accession card read "sample
obtained in 1903 by Mr. E. B. Collins of a paper used in the library
of the home of Mark Twain, Hartford, Connecticut. Installed by
Tiffany decorators." Period photographs of the Clemens library
clearly established that this was not the library paper. Because the
sample was in reds, golds and browns, because the library and the
dining room of the Hartford house open on to each other, and
because the paper was similar to other period dining room papers,
it was decided that this probably was the original Clemens dining
room paper.

The paper itself is of rampant lilies complete with tendrils and
leaves, the pattern created by low embossing, and then covered with
a gilt and lacquer finish in dark brown. The paper had a straight
repeat, drop match. In the plaster wall, on either side of the north
window of the Dining Room, the original Tiffany glass panels survived. In 1968 while checking the room for evidence prior to
restoration, it was decided to remove these Tiffany panels to see if
any important clues were behind them. The entire fireplace was
photographed and then the moldings which held the glass panels in
place were removed and numbered. It is crucial to photograph,
measure and number a site and its parts before and during investigation. Months and years may elapse before re-installation and
one's memory is not always reliable. Finally, the first glass panel was
removed and there, behind it, but there intact, was a large sample
of wallpaper. It was the same embossed paper which was in the
Cooper-Hewitt collection. Behind every panel more wallpaper was
found. Tiffany had believed that the 1874 mantel "could not be
made to look well" with his 1881 decorations and it had been
removed.[4] If the new mantel and overmantel arrangement had not
been ready in time, the decorators would have completely papered
the wall and then later put in the mantel. In this way the Tiffany
mantel would have covered the Tiffany wallpaper. The positions of
the fragments and its elements were carefully recorded so that when
the paper was reproduced the reproduction would hang precisely
where the original had hung.

In the case of the Dining Room wallpaper it was necessary, after recording all the evidence, to remove it from the wall to preserve it. It was mounted on 100 percent acid free rag board. If a paper is backed with a muslin, then removal is relatively simple, requiring only gently easing a flat putty knife behind the muslin to release the muslin from the wall. When a paper has been pasted directly onto the plaster wall, extreme care is necessary. Many Victorian papers were printed with water soluble colors, hence wetting of the papers to soften the paste will also destroy the pigments. The most practicable method is carefully to steam off the paper, proceeding slowly, section by section. When a section has been removed, it should be placed between white blotters which will absorb the moisture but will do minimum damage to the colors.*

There are times when finding an original paper such as Mark Twain's Dining Room paper is both thrilling and terrible. "Terrible" because the reproduction of this dining room paper obviously was going to be a very complex and lengthy procedure. Even if the techniques and craftsmen could be found, it would still require enormous time, money and perseverance. Aware of the obstacles, the Committee proceeded with the task of reproducing the paper. First, a complete spectographic analysis was made to determine, if possible, the nature of the paper and the composition of the colors. Colors fade and discolor with age and it is imperative to know, for example, if the gold color was produced by gold leaf, a composition dutch metal leaf, or a bronze paint. Analysis revealed that the gold colored area was indeed a dutch metal leaf. In places the leaf was completely covered by a dark red color, and the iron found in the analysis could have been used as the base for the red pigment. The analysis also detected the presence of aluminum, calcium, some copper, magnesium, manganese, silica and titanium. Unfortunately, the results were far from definitive, except that leaf, not a bronze paint, had been used.

At this point the Committee proceeded to investigate the possibility of having the paper reproduced. Several firms were ap-

---

*Once in a New York house the author found that steaming would not budge the paper he desired. Faced with the need to have the paper but being unable to steam it cleanly from the wall he sectioned the paper off and removed the entire wall. To this day he has not been able to work the paper from the plaster, and though it is extremely bulky, he has successfully preserved the wallpaper design he wanted.

The full scale drawing of the wallpaper from which the embossing rollers were created.

proached about reproducing the wallpaper. Most proposed hand-screening the design on a textured brown vinyl. The cost of this process was relatively inexpensive, but the effect was unfortunate. It presented the pattern but not the embossed impression and the Committee felt that embossed relief was vital to the overall design and effect. The next step was to find a firm to make the rollers which would exactly reproduce the original pattern. Larsen Design Studio of New York said in 1968 they could have the rollers made for an accurate reproduction. Modern wallpaper rollers are not made of the same size as was the original paper. To overcome this obstacle, a full scale drawing of the paper was made, with the repeat. Because of the rollers, the design was modified but the scale and feeling was retained. After reviewing the embossed proofs, the white embossed paper was ordered, unfinished.

Unfortunately, neither Larsen nor any other firm could sat-

After sealing the paper, each sheet was sized and covered with a
dutch metal leaf.

To cover the paper with a rich ox blood glaze yet leave the flowers in
gold, a stencil was cut.

isfactorily machine-finish the paper, so the Memorial temporarily
stored the embossed unfinished paper. Trustee Henry Darbee, after
many hours of research and experimentation, devised a procedure
which would satisfactorily reproduce the colors. It involved some
seven steps and was done entirely by hand. Master craftsmen Leo-
pold and Bernhard Sans, of Sans Painting and Decorating, who
had worked with the Restoration Committee from 1966, then proceeded to hand finish the paper by this method. Each roll was measured for its place in the room. Then, working flat on tables, the
master painters applied a sealer to protect the embossing. Sheet
after sheet was then sized and the dutch metal applied over the entire surface. When the sheets had thoroughly dried, a stencil was
cut and an oxblood red glaze was applied exactly where it had appeared in the original. At this point the paper was hung on the walls
and covered with three layers of a clear finish tinted with burnt
umber. Hand wiping after each layer was undertaken to produce
highlights. Slowly the garish red and gold changed to look like em-

Handwiping produced the necessary highlights in the paper.

bossed leather. One visitor on seeing the half-finished wall, one side bright and modern with the gold and red, the other glazed much darker, commented "It's amazing how they can clean off all that grime and get down to the beautiful red and gold." The glazing was necessary to reproduce the 1881 paper. When the room was finished Committee members sighed with relief, and one member said, "It seems to call back our grandfathers."

An original sideboard was returned to the Memorial by the Waterman family of Hartford, the original dining room table came back from New Jersey, and two of the original chairs were returned from a demolition contractor. On the center of the table in 1977 there is a great silver epergne, laden with fruit, as it was the day that Samuel Langhorne Clemens and Olivia Langdon were married. The deep wine red portieres, the rich leather upholstered chairs, the wallpaper of lilies, all combine to give the room elegance and warmth as the table with its gold and white china, and its silver and crystal, invoke a sparkle and a gaiety once so familiar in this room:

*The Dining Room when it served as the main charging room for the
public library and the same room restored.*

10

Library

"One of the pleasantest neighborhood customs that grew up in the Hartford home was the gathering of an evening, around the library fire while Mr. Clemens read aloud: He liked stirring poetry, which he read admirably, sometimes rousing his little audience to excitement and cheers."[1]

The Library was central to the life of the Clemens family. Here they would gather before or after dinner to hear Mark Twain read aloud from his newly completed manuscripts for family approval or censorship. Here the father rough-housed with his daughters, sometimes on wild tiger hunts in pursuit of George, the butler. The anecdotes which came from this room are numerous: the story of the snake which crawled in one winter afternoon only to be apprehended by the author and flung out the alcove door, the dinner party which voted not to disband until the genial morn appeared, and the midnight wassail sung in the library.

The room was dominated by a great mantel which had been purchased by the Clemenses in Scotland in 1874. A contemporary of the Clemens children remembered the mantel as "covered with garlands that spring forth in plastic rotundity and clamber along the edges."[2] All along the sides of the library were bookshelves, but the bookshelves on either side of the mantel had a special arrangement, a procession of ornaments, paintings and bric-a-brac.

As often as they could, the Clemens children would require their father to tell them a story, a romance, always beginning with the oil portrait of a cat in a ruff and including every item, every ornament, in turn, until one reached the impressionist water color of a beautiful young girl, whom the family called Emmeline. Day after day, a new story full of violence and bloodshed, but always in order. When Olivia's mother, Mrs. Langdon, visited, she sat in the rocker by the fireplace and made pin cushions and emories. When the

The Library when it served as the adult reading room for the public library. The mantel is the 1903 replacement mantel.

children dramatized *The Prince and the Pauper* as a surprise for their father, they performed it in the Library.

In 1881 the Associated Artists stenciled the library in peacock blue with metallic designs. With the rich dark wood of the bookcases and the mantel, and the red velvet draperies and lambrequins, the room has a resplendent, evocative atmosphere. Over the fireplace opening was a brass shield on which was inscribed "The ornament of a house is the friends who frequent it." So aptly did the motto describe the house.

When Mark Twain sold the house in 1903, he took the great Scottish mantel with him. Mrs. Bissell completely redecorated the Library, covering the walls with grass cloth, placing small electric sconces here and there. Later, the Library served as the study hall for Kingswood boys, and then, when the apartments came in, there

The Library in 1875, shortly after the Clemenses moved in.

was the painful, negative noise of hammers ripping out all the original bookcases. In 1955, the Library was a big empty room, a skeleton of its former self. Guides who escorted visitors through the room recounted the former glory of the house, of the plays performed in the room, of the author rough-housing with his children, of the stories told about the ornaments on either side of the lost Scottish mantel. "Mark Twain had later installed the mantel in his home 'Stormfield' in Redding, Connecticut. 'Stormfield' was destroyed by fire in 1923. Someday we may be able to have a duplicate, a facsimile, made." One visitor, Mr. Lawrence Banks, asked "Was it a big mantel with a shield and knight's helmet and fruit and flowers?" As a matter of fact, it was. "Well," Mr. Banks went on, "In my father's barn we have a mantel which came from 'Stormfield.' It's in pieces but it sounds like the same one." Could it be?!

Trustee James Thomson immediately went to the barn in Redding and there in pieces, but there, amid the hay and harnesses, was the great Hartford mantel. It was returned to the Mark Twain house in Hartford. Carefully cleaned and repaired, it was installed in 1958. It has been this kind of luck which has made the impossible not only seem possible, but reasonable.

In the summer of 1963 while cleaning one of the basement rooms, an intern found an interesting piece of scroll carving. It was not very big but, because it was interesting, he showed it to the Director. This scroll turned out to be part of the carving from one of the original Library bookcases. With this piece to give an accurate scale and a second piece already in the Memorial's possession, with the photos and the profiles marked on the floor and walls, there was enough information to have the original cases reproduced. Drawings were made of each bookcase. Because of the cost, first the basic bookcases were commissioned, and then, six years later, money was available for the stretcher carvings, and finally two years later the corner brackets were carved. All of the carvings were done by Mr. Edwin A. Dressel of Cheshire, Connecticut.

Work on the restoration of the walls and ceiling of the Library was begun in 1968. Contemporaries of the Clemenses remembered the stenciled design as being blue and silver. When we carefully scraped through the layers of paint, what was revealed was a strong peacock blue and gold. The design was the same as those in early

*Mark Twain in his last home in Redding, with the lower part of the
Scottish mantel behind him.*

photographs of the room. A sample of the wall and of the ceiling
was, therefore, cut out and run through a spectrograph to determine if the colors were, indeed, gold and blue, and if the gold was
gold leaf or paint. Analysis revealed that no silver or tin or nickel or

The Drawing Room restored.

The Dining Room wallpaper before the dark glaze was applied.

The Dining Room wallpaper with the dark glaze being hand wiped.

The mastercraftsmen hand finishing the wallpaper.

The Dining Room restored.

The east wall of the Library with the great Scottish mantel.

The Library looking south to the Conservatory.

The Mahogany guest room restored.

similar material used to give a silver effect was present, and that the gold was a bronze paint. As before, every detail was recorded, preserved and then reproduced. The room was resplendent with its gold and blue, and some members wondered how anyone could have mistaken the gold for silver. The question was answered, by chance, when walking through the room one afternoon someone noticed the effect the west light had on the walls. The late sun streaming across the walls turned them to silver. It would have been this stunning effect which contemporaries remembered as they waited with the family at tea or before going in to dinner.

In investigating the ceiling, two gas outlets were discovered, one in the center of the room, where a gas chandelier was pictured in an 1874 photograph, and one to the west of that outlet by some two feet. When the electrified chandelier was removed, the 1881 Tiffany designs were found beneath. The second, or newly discovered outlet, (which never had been electrified) was clearly incorporated in the stenciled designs. Further investigation found traces of the rosette seen in the 1875 photograph around the first chandelier location. This evidence indicated that the first chandelier location was changed by Tiffany to the second location. In 1903, when the house was electrified, the chandelier was moved back to the first location. To be accurate to the 1881 period, the chandelier was moved to the Tiffany location.

Is the placement of a chandelier or any lighting fixture that important and worth all this effort? Regrettably, one of the most overlooked factors in any restoration is lighting, the type of fixture and the power of the illumination.

Organizations will spend a great deal of time, energy and money restoring a house, or in the case of a museum, setting up a period room, working on the walls, the ceilings, purchasing or acquiring the proper paintings, sculpture, decorative arts, only to bring in modern spotlights and reduce the setting to one of medical textbook clarity and insensitivity. Light is probably the single most important factor in the creation or recreation of a mood. To present a room accurately, the natural and artificial light in that room must receive special attention.

By the 1870's gas light was the basic means of artificial light. It was supplemented by earlier forms of lighting, oil, kerosene and

The children of Mr. Lawrence Banks with the rediscovered mantel in the Redding barn.

candles. But gas light never had the intensity or the sharpness of electric light. Gas was dirty and unreliable. The following was written by Mark Twain to the Hartford Gas Company:

"Dear Sirs: Some day you will move me almost to the verge of irritation by your chuckle headed Goddamned fashion of shutting your Goddamned gas off without giving any notice to your Goddamned parishioners. Several times you have come within an ace of smothering half of this household in their beds and blowing up the other half by this idiotic, not to say criminal, custom of yours. And it has happened again today. Haven't you a telephone?"³

But gas light was more convenient and brighter than candles. Due to romantic movies, we expect gas light to be brilliant. It was not. Those who do not agree with this statement only have to look carefully at the portrait of the Hatch Family by Eastman Johnson, which is in the Metropolitan Museum of Art in New York. The room is illuminated by gas, and appears to be a comfortable atmosphere with sufficient light. But is there enough light? If there were, why is the grandfather almost hanging out the window in order to get enough light to read the paper.

The most frequent compliment that visitors give the Mark Twain house is that they feel as if the family did actually live there, in fact, as if they had just left the room. The most frequent complaint: "I can't see." Mark Twain once wrote "outside it was as dark and dreary as if the world had been lit with Hartford Gas."⁴ In choosing the tint for a room, Associated Artists did so with particular reference "to the quantity and quality of light which pervades it." They did not know of, nor decorate it for, 150 watt bulbs. Unfortunately, the Hartford Gas Company and the insurance agent would not allow the restoration to illuminate the house by gaslight. After a great deal of searching a manufacturer was found who presented an alternate solution. Marketed by Angelo Brothers, the small, tubular bulbs are covered with Welsbach mantels which, when controlled by dimmers, create the proper effect. By day the window shades, the curtains, draperies and lambrequins filter out the light. By night the light is soft, with the metallic stenciled designs of Associated Artists moving, shaping the spaces. By day the Library is well lit by the natural light which streams in from the south and west. At night the chandelier, placed off center by Mr. Tiffany, illuminates the room and the bay, evenly lighting the walls. This effect would not have been possible if the chandelier were in the center of the room.

Slowly, the Library has resumed its original appearance. The mantel has returned, and back in place are the bookshelves, the painting of the cat in a ruff, the bracket gas lamps, and the table lamps which provided enough light for reading. So many afternoons and evenings were spent here, by Mark Twain and his family

One of the original brackets from the Library bookshelves.

and his friends, talking and especially listening to Mark Twain read aloud from Browning, from Shakespeare, or from a recently completed manuscript. It was in this room, as Twain read the draft of Huckleberry Finn aloud to the family, that Huck's being combed "all to hell" was edited by Livy to read "all to thunder." On another afternoon Livy heard a great commotion in this room and investigated. There was Twain convulsed with laughter over a book he was reading. She asked the title and he said he did not know, he had merely picked it off the shelf. Glancing over his shoulder, Livy discovered that the book he was enjoying so thoroughly was one by Mark Twain.[5]

The great mantel, the carved bookcases laden with books and newspapers, the deep-cushioned lounges, all invite the visitor to pause and to read. It is a reasonable space created in an era and for a family which reserved some room for reading, for conversation, for the spirited exchange of ideas.

The Library as it appeared in an 1885 issue of Harpers' and the restoration.

11

Conservatory

At the south end of the Library is a wonderful bower of bliss, a little semi-circular Conservatory. William Dean Howells recalled: "The plants were set in the ground, and the flowering vines climbed up the sides and overhung the roof above the silent spray of a fountain companied by callas and other water-loving lilies. There, while we breakfasted, Patrick came in from the barn and sprinkled the pretty bower, which poured out its responsive perfume in the delicate accents of its waned blossoms."[1] It is a dramatic vista, looking from the Dining Room, through the Library to that sunny, Japanese-lanterned retreat.

Like every other area in the house, the Conservatory underwent many changes after the Clemenses sold the house. In 1903 Mrs. Bissell transformed it into a fashionable fernery, with a cement floor replacing the marble chip path, and shelves and brackets to hold the ferns. Later the glass roof was taken out and replaced by one of wood and rolled roofing. During the Kingswood School period, students learned to play bridge in this area; later it served as an apartment kitchen. In 1962, the Trustees decided to restore the Conservatory in memory of Margaret E. Graves, Curator from 1954 until 1961. Friends of Miss Graves contributed the necessary funds for this project, but no commemorative plaque was installed, nor have any such plaques been installed in the house. This was the well-considered decision of the Restoration Committee, feeling that the house was Mark Twain's home, and not an exhibition area. As Mark Twain did not have plaques, they would be inappropriate in the restoration. Full recognition and acknowledgment is made through detailed permanent records that do not detract from the convincing honesty of the work.

There were only two visual sources on which to base the restoration of the Conservatory. The first was a stereopticon slide

Mrs. Richard Bissel with Anne-Caroline, Richard and William in the Conservatory in 1909.

taken in 1875, one year after the house was built, showing a marble chip path encircling the bubble fountain, and a very modest compliment of plants. The other source was a sketch by Childe Hassam published in *Harper's Monthly Magazine,* May, 1896. The Hassam sketch showed a shade across the top of the Conservatory entrance, several Japanese lanterns, and so great a profusion of plants that no view was to be had of the Conservatory itself. In 1891 the Clemens family went to Europe, but Patrick, their gardener, was left in charge, and the Hassam sketch shows the fruits of his labors.

With these two visual clues, the Restoration was begun by excavation of the area. Beneath the "modern" cement floor was found

The Conservatory in 1875 with its modest compliment of plants.

the original marble path, proof that it was indeed marble and the actual size of the chips was documented. Also uncovered in the excavation was one of the original cast iron plant brackets which had been on either side of the door, and a fragment of a doll's dress. Later scraping of the doorways determined the exact placement for the brackets. Though the original glass roof had been replaced, the original wood structure survived beneath the "modern" wooden roof. City safety regulations prohibited the reinstallation of a glass roof. After considerable debate, permission was obtained to install a roof of clear plexiglass. In covering small areas, plexiglass is an ideal substitute when glass cannot be used. (Safety glass with the wire mesh or similar supportive material is not desirable as the wire will severely detract from the desired visual presentation.)

The bubble nozzle for the fountain was obtained from a local nurseryman, and the fountain was put on a recirculating pump to to reduce the water bill.

A small radiator with a separate thermostat was discreetly installed along the east wall to keep the plants from freezing in the winter.

From the beginning the Restoration Committee felt that all the plants in the Conservatory and in the house must be of the period, and where identifiable, those known to have been in the Clemens conservatory. Mary Edwards, noted landscape architect and Trustee of the Memorial, supervised and nurtured the Conservatory beginning in 1963. The beginning was extremely modest due to lack of funds and because no solid research had been done on the plants known to have been used in Victorian conservatories prior to 1891. As Mary Edwards recalled, the early restoration plantings included "a borrowed rubber tree, a banana planted in an ash can disguised by carpeting, and ferns retrieved from under poinsettias."[2] Research revealed that the donated luxuriant asparagus ferns were too late for this house and had to be removed. Tiny slips of the creeping fig (*Ficus Repens*) were grown by Trustee Robert H. Schutz, the grandson of Mark Twain's physician, Dr. Cincinnatus A. Taft. These were no ordinary slips, at least not to the Committee, but the descendants of the very creeping fig which Mrs. Clemens had grown originally in the Conservatory.

Mary Edwards, Sally Capozzoli, Inez Goltra and others re-

Childe Hassam's sketch of the Conservatory.

searched the plants which were known and used during this period.
Trips to Boston and the Massachusetts Horticultural Society produced a long list of Victorian conservatory favorites, some known
and some virtually impossible to find. The Memorial owns Mrs.
Clemens' copy of Peter Henderson's *Practical Floriculture* and her
father's copy of Henderson's *Handbook of Plants*. These became the
standard reference books, along with Shirley Hibberts' *New and
Rare Beautiful-Leaved Plants* (1870) which also documented the
proper pots and containers for period plants. Periodicals, photographs of other Victorian houses, bills from local nurserymen,
newspaper advertisements and trade cards aided in forming the

body of reference material. With the assumption that Mrs. Clemens, encouraged by Patrick, might have chosen period double flowers over single, and variegated white or reddish leaves over green, such specimens were selected. In 1969, a snapshot of the Childe Hassam view was discovered in an old Hartford photograph album. It had been taken by a sixteen year old boy in 1896 and brought into focus the impressionistic lines of the artist. Clearly visible are the potted aspidistra, the rubber trees, the large leaved zebra plant (*Calthea Zebrine*) and the pots of *Columnea Schiecleana* set in the cast iron brackets on the side of the doorway. Where possible, these have been placed in their documented location.

In 1977 the Conservatory was resplendent with plants. Around the fountain and the circular path were baby's tears and selaginella, begonias, fittonias, variegated spiderwort and pittosporum, colorful gymnostachyms, marantas and crotons. Along the wood braces and roof two of the 184 possible species of the passion flower vine (*Passiflora caerulea* and *Passiflora alata*) grow luxuriantly. Hoya carnosa blooms sweetly and grows well when the soil around it can be kept dry. The Bougainvillea climbed to join the original creeping fig, and the Bird of Paradise and Clivia bloom. The large pink trumpet-shaped flowers of the *Dipladeniasplendens* surprised many visitors. Hymenocallis and nightblooming cereus provided nocturnal but brief scents. With regret, one may recall William Dean Howells' remembrance of the delicious fragrance of the sweet olive (*Osmanthus fragrans*) which in 1977 barely floated into the Library, and never reached to the Dining Room.

One of the main problems of presenting a Conservatory such as Mark Twain's is that it must be on display year round. In Victorian times such conservatories were emptied in the summer. Since that is not possible, the plants endure under less than ideal conditions. Under the summer sun it is often as hot as 90° in there, and the great towering beech tree to the south casts the plants in shade. The documented nasturtiums will not bloom for the lack of sun. Other plants such as the screw pine (*Pandanus utilis*) are seven feet tall, and the rubber plants must be topped to prevent them from pushing through the roof.

In Mark Twain's day there was a working greenhouse across the lawn which provided the required profusion of blooms or the

At sixteen Thomas Russell photographed the Conservatory in 1896.

appropriate seasonal splashes of color. In 1977 donated or purchased Poinsettias, Chrysanthemums, hyacinths and tulips provided the seasonal color. At Christmas, Robert Gregus would bring
in his majestic yellow jasmines which bloom through the season, to
be followed by his great tubs of period orchids. Members and
friends board plants on the off season, and when the plants begin to
blossom, return them to the Conservatory for all to enjoy. In this
way, lacking the Clemens' greenhouse, or the funds to purchase
plants, or to hire a full-time Patrick, the present Conservatory is
able to be presented with the care and profusion of its earliest days.

12

Mahogany Guest Suite

On the ground floor of the house, off the Library, was a guest room. William Dean Howells called it "a royal chamber" and his young son, John Mead Howells, marveled at the room's appointments and conveniences, right down to the red soap which John called "painted." To the family it was the Mahogany Guest Room, because its "furniture and parts of the walls were of this wood."[1] The room is spacious and comfortable and has a separate dressing room and separate bathroom. The bathroom is complete with sinks, toilet, tub and shower. At Christmas the room became the wrapping room and the storeroom for presents. When the children were presenting a play for their parents or guests it served as the green room. It was here that Mark Twain had the control box for his burglar alarm, though he would usually disconnect it at night "so the family should not be aroused if anybody tried to get in at the window."[2] It was to this room that Susy Clemens was brought in August, 1896, when she was stricken with spinal meningitis. Katy Leary, the family maid, described the scene:

> "Mr. Langdon came to Hartford in the morning and we took her over to the old home. She was very sick and she wouldn't take a bit of medicine from anybody but me. She wouldn't let the nurses touch her or come near her, so I sat by her night and day—night and day, I sat. Oh it was a terrible time. My heart aches even now when I think of it, after all these years. Poor little Susy! She died before we even could sail."[3]

When the house was saved in 1929, the Mahogany Guest Suite served as the offices, the exhibit area, the storage area. The offices were moved upstairs to the nursery area in 1956, and with the acquisition of the original bed and dresser, the room began to assume some of its original character. Tours were small, but without fail in the Mahogany bathroom a cub scout would turn the knob to the shower and drench a companion. Therefore, to protect the house from leaking pipes or overflowing sinks, all the plumbing in the main part of the house was disconnected.

In 1968, beneath the molding of the room, were found scraps of wallpaper, a pine needle design in yellow, pink and blue on an ecru background, highlighted with gold sunbursts. Other fragments of the same paper were found rolled up behind the door frames in the dressing room. It was similar to wallpapers designed by Tiffany in 1879 and reproduced in Warren & Fuller's "What Should We Do with Our Walls?" Two members of the Restoration Committee, Henry Darbee and the author, working independently, struggled to reconstruct the pattern from these few fragments. When they were finished, they compared their separate drawings and found them to be the same. Because the reconstructed pattern was very similar to other aesthetic papers, because it was probably from the period when the Associated Artists decorated the room, because it was all the evidence which survived and yet gave the rooms a grace and style which was entirely in keeping with period accounts, the Restoration Committee voted to have the reconstructed wallpaper design reproduced. Though no evidence survived of the ceiling decorations, Tiffany's 1881 contract had stated "ceiling painted or papered at our option." For the ceiling the Committee elected merely to double strike the gold sunburst pattern and use it as a ceiling paper.

The door between the guest room and its dressing room was a sliding door in 1968. Yet it, and the door jamb, bore the unmistakable indication that the doors had been hinged. When was it changed? Some felt that it was unlikely that the Clemenses would have changed it, and surely the sliding arrangement must be a "Bissellism" or later. Others weren't so sure. Carefully, the door was removed to see if the track bore a manufacturer's name, a patent date, anything. It did not. But, under one end, way in the back, was a small piece of newspaper, which the carpenter had used to shim up the track. Carefully, the newspaper was unfolded. On one side was an advertisement for "Knox the Hatters" at No. 194 Fifth Avenue and No. 212 Broadway, New York. On the other side an advertisement for an A. Werner & Co. of Broadway, New York for vintage 1879 champagne. We wrote the New York Historical Society asking them if they could date this fragment. Mr. James J. Heslin

Discovered beneath the sliding track, these clippings made possible the dating of the door arrangement.

replied "we think the newspaper evidently dates from 1882 or 1883. A. Werner & Company moved from the address shown late in 1883 or early 1884." More likely it was from 1881-2 when Louis C. Tiffany and Associated Artists redecorated the room. Careful on-site investigation had provided persuasive evidence and the door was put back on its sliding track.

In many houses, evidence and treasures survive because no one has ripped them out. In the dressing room, (a room Clara Clemens remembered as the perfect place to study at six a.m. "as it was warmer than any other place,") the fireplace was covered by layers and layers of paint.[4] When the paint was removed, there, protected, but in place, were the original tiles. Removal of the mortar backing of the fireplace disclosed a period cast iron backing with a charming design of figures and mythological animals. There was a gas jet in the corner which corresponded with Clara's notation, "gas stove fireplace."

On the Dressing Room walls, beneath the layers of paint and paper were found cartoons drawn on the plaster. These drawings consisted of a trellis and arch designs, with a frieze of cattails, sketches for flowers and in places someone had written "mirror here," "white," "37 High St." and other comments. Who had drawn the cartoons and made the notations? Architect Edward T. Potter, a builder, later occupants? The Connecticut State Police were called, and after they determined our request was not another crank call, Lt. George Fagan of the Identification Bureau and Anthony Liberi, Chief Identification Technician came to see the walls. They felt the writing was clear enough to identify and later Lt. Paul Seaman came with Mr. Liberi to photograph the samples. Copies of original letters by Mr. Potter in 1875 were given to them. The results of their Handwriting Examination were:

> "**Exhibits**: Q-1: photographs of writing that appears on uncovered plaster walls at the Mark Twain Memorial in Hartford.
> K-1: copies of letter written by Edward Tuckerman Potter dating from 1875.
>
> **Findings**: Examination of Q-1 and comparison with K-1 reveals that all distinguishable writing in the brown crayon or paint, "mirror here," "white," etc. confirms to the known writing of Edward Tuckerman Potter, and can be accepted as having been written by him. The pencil writing, "37 High St." etc. differs from Potter's writing and was not written by him."

The report was approved by Captain Albert H. Pethick.

At this time the plaster walls were completely removed for preservation. As there was no indication that Mr. Potter's design was ever carried out in this space, the Committee voted to wallpaper the space with the paper which had been found here and in the adjoining bedroom.

The original bed and dresser were returned to the house in

The cartoons which survived beneath layers of paint and paper.

1956. Their elegantly refined lines, highlighted by English tiles, speak of the grandeur of the room. The gold sunbursts in the wall and ceiling papers subtly reflect the activity, even the commotion, which once filled the space; guests arriving with luggage that had to be carried in and unpacked, Livy carefully wrapping dozens of Christmas presents for family and friends, the Clemens girls and their friends scurrying around, changing costumes or rehearsing lines for another family theatrical, and, also, the tragic afternoon when Susy was carried here, too sick to sail to join the family in England.

13

Master Bedroom

At the top of the stairs on the second floor is the Master Bedroom. In the early fifties the room was no longer rented as an apartment, but opened as an exhibition area where, for twenty-five cents, one could see the growing collection of Mark Twain memorabilia. The room was also an early target for restoration. Clara Clemens' floor plans indicated the placement of the bed, dressers, and desk. She recalled that the decorations gave "an impression of a rather sombre, bluish green color, though not of a peacock or turquoise shade." On top of one of the door casings, rolled up by a scraping tool, a tiny scrap of wallpaper was discovered, resembling a green "tea" paper in two shades of green with brown and gold. It corresponded with Clara's recollection, but unfortunately the fragment was too small for accurate reconstruction of the paper. Researchers checked every possible wallpaper collection, in the hope that this fragment would correspond with a larger sample, thus making possible reconstruction of the paper. To date, no sample has been found.

In 1974 scraping of the ceiling revealed stenciled designs around the central rosette and in the border. No color was discernible except in the plaster rosette where a green was indicated (similar to that in the wallpaper) highlighted with gold stripes. This color was used for the ceiling, and the stenciling was reproduced in a corresponding color. The background color of the original paper fragment was used for the walls. Still, the search continues — somewhere there must survive interior photographs of the house, and of this room, which will solve the puzzle and offer a detailed solution.

In 1977, as in 1878, the room was dominated by the great walnut bed which Mark Twain purchased in Venice. During the Hartford period, Mark and Livy slept with their heads at the foot of the bed. Thus, they could admire the elaborately carved headboard; there was a second reason—the many protruding elbows, arms and toes produced by the heavily carved putti would have made sitting up in bed with the headboard as a back rest extremely uncomfortable. This great bed is the same landmark in which

Sam Clemens writing in 1906 in the great Venetian bed.

Twain dictated his autobiography with one of the putti on the columns viewing the day's work. It is also the bed in which Twain was
so often photographed, and in which, on April 21, 1910, the day
after the reappearance in the sky of Halley's comet, he died.

Beside the bed is an extension gas light, its umbilical cord carrying the fuel from the central chandelier, for reading at night.
Mark Twain's daughter returned the bed to the house in 1940.
Later, an original dresser, the desk owned by Mark Twain's
mother, and even Livy's porcelain clock were returned. On the
mantel and beside the dresser and desk are family photographs,
family mementoes, and a drawing of a robin, the State bird of Connecticut, created by Susy and Jean Clemens. When they were sick,
the daughters might sleep in this room, in the great bed. On a quiet
afternoon Susy, Clara and Jean would slip into the room and remove one of the putti from the columns and powder and bathe it as
though it were a little doll.

For the putti the quiet of the three girls must have been a
remarkable change from the mornings when Mark Twain hurled
buttonless shirts out of the bathroom window. The shirts would
float to the rhododendron below, to the accompaniment of a spirited stream of oaths which any riverboatman, miner or newspaperman would have recognized and endorsed. Twain possessed a
full range of intense and conflicting emotions. Livy Clemens
understood her husband; she called him "Youth" and theirs was a
happy and close relationship. Her delicate features, her extremely
capable mind, her patience, and the loving household she created
for Samuel Clemens, greatly affected his writing. Far removed from
the public rooms on the first floor, and even removed from their
daughters' rooms and the guest rooms, was this, their private
retreat, where husband and wife could be alone and together.

14

Schoolroom

When Mark Twain first moved into the Hartford house in 1874, the large room on the second floor, adjoining the nursery on the southwest side, was his study. With its many windows overlooking the quiet river and distant hill, with the great, comfortable divan which he had had copied from a Syrian monastery, with so many distractions, he found he could not concentrate. He preferred to recline on the divan and watch the passing of the seasons, an ice storm, robins building a nest, almost anything but work. Eventually, Mark Twain moved his desk to the Billiard Room on the third floor and there he placed it where he could see only a wall and shelves of books. His old study became the schoolroom for his daughters and their contemporaries in the neighborhood. Clara recalled: "Our schoolroom provided memories never to be repeated. Snowstorms raging about the many windows, against which a fire on the hearth cozily defended us. And our Shakespeare club! Oh, the wonderful plays we produced with a larger cast of actors than auditors! Memory tests of books we had read and hated. Recitations of poetry we adored. Concerts performed on our baby upright. But, best of all, popcorn and roasted chestnuts. All these royal pleasures in a room modestly called the schoolroom."[1]

In 1971 the room lacked all of the charm and romance Clara Clemens described. The last tenant had moved out in 1968 and the room had served as the work room and Board Room and storage room. Its walls and woodwork were a dingy green, its hearth black from soot and paint. Restoration, or the investigation for the restoration, began with the cleaning of the hearth. Beneath the paint, marvelous tiles of oak leaves in soft browns came to light.

Again, using the standard procedure, there began investigation of the walls and the woodwork. Beneath layers of green and cream and red paint could be found bits and pieces of a stencil design, with swags and rosettes. It corresponded with the patterns discovered on the ceiling. There was enough of the design to reconstruct it with some accuracy, and using the fragments and period books, an estimate of the original colors could be made.

While debate continued on the design, the craftsmen proceeded to investigate the woodwork. It was oak, and originally had had a clear finish. The many coats of paint were removed from the oak paneling.

In the north-east corner of the room, there was a closet door, not oak but pine. This pine had all of the later coats of paint. Was it possible that when Mrs. Bissell remodeled the Clemens' schoolroom to make her bedroom, that she had had this door cut into the hall closet? If so, it was more than possible that the alterations were done before the redecorating of the room, and that beneath the door casement, protected by the pine, were fragments of the original designs. Very, very slowly the molding and the framing for the door were loosened from the wall. Carefully they were removed, and there it was! Pristine and protected across the years the complete pattern of the walls survived, the colors clean and crisp.

A skeptic might ask whether the stencil designs on the wall and the matching design under the pine woodwork were definitely of the Clemens' period. A check of all the walls, and all must be checked to locate the original designs, revealed the outlets for the original gas fixtures. These were covered with plaster plugs which were painted with the green, cream and red paint found on top of the stenciled designs. On the gas plugs there were no layers of paint below the red. Red was also the first layer on the woodwork. On removing the plugs, it was found that one of them had newspaper as wadding. This paper was carefully unfolded and found to bear the date 1903, the year the Bissells purchased the house and electrified it. Thus, it was conclusive that the installation of the new door and the elimination of the gas lights had occurred at the same time. What lay beneath the red, beneath the door, was the Clemens period.

Once again, the schoolroom appears as if its busy young occupants had just left the room, interrupted by some excitement in another corner of the house. The painted fans which Mark Twain gave his daughters hang over the upright piano. Volumes of *Little*

The original design survived beneath a "modern" door frame.

Women, Black Beauty, Jules Verne and the Bodley's adventures
line the shelves. On the tables and chairs are other books, toys, an
unfinished macrame project, and a pile of stereopticons. In the
alcove is a pile of elegant grownup gowns. It was a favorite pastime
of Susy Clemens and her playmate, Margret Warner, to act out
their history lessons, especially the confrontation between the quar-
reling Queens, Elizabeth and Mary Queen of Scots. Their father
spied on them once; he marveled at the eloquent four syllable
words, dripping with blood, which the monarchs spoke as they
strode around the room, dragging several feet of gown behind
them. Young Jean Clemens had a very special part in these high
dramas, namely, to sit at a low table and to compose death warrants for one of the Queens to sign. If there was a long period between death warrants, Jean would calmly put her head on the table
and quietly go to sleep.

15

Nursery

"Two of us, Jean and I, slept in the nursery, and my elder sister Susy, occupied the little blue room adjoining."[1] Thus Clara Clemens described the children's area of the second floor. The Nursery later served as the bedroom for Richard M. Bissell, Jr., then as an apartment, then as offices for the growing Memorial in 1957. When one entered this door in 1963, immediately on the right there was a fireplace, so immediate, in fact, that if one closed the door by using its side and not the knob, one's fingers would be painfully caught between the door and the mantel. (A mistake seldom repeated.) Straight ahead were the bookshelves for the Memorial's growing reference library, two desks, a mimeograph machine and four file cabinets, a cupboard, a sink, a pile of "in" and "out" baskets, and a long table for the Board of Trustees. The quarters were extremely cramped, but there was work to do, and the director, the secretary, and the many volunteers seemed to make the best of the situation and, more remarkably, to get their work done.

By March, 1968, things had improved slightly. The School-room apartment which adjoined the Nursery was no longer rented, and it became the "board room." Susy's room became the research room, and the children's bath, with facilities removed, became the Director's office.

In restoring the Clemens' Nursery, the only known solid evidence other than the placement of furniture, was that the Bissell family in 1903 had painted the room "a strong blue." Beneath layer after layer of paint there were found traces of this blue, but little else. One afternoon in March, 1968, Committee members began to investigate the aforementioned treacherous mantel. The upper mantel was pried away from the wall and there behind it was a child's wallpaper with block designs of animals, frogs and mice and ducks and cats, alternating with floral designs. The colors in the paper compared favorably with those found in period children's books.

Often, when a room is papered, the trim and mantels are eased forward, making it possible for the decorator to slip the paper behind the wood, thus avoiding intricate cut lines. When the room was redecorated in 1903, the workmen who stripped the walls had not bothered to remove the mantel thus preserving this early sample. The "strong blue" paint had dribbled behind the mantel and on top of the paper. As this paper was under the paint, there could be no doubt that it was Clemens period.

Mrs. Catherine Frangiamore, formerly of the Cooper-Hewitt Museum and later Curator of the Atlanta Historical Society, identified the paper as Walter Crane's 1877 "Nursery Rhymes Design" or "Ye Frog He Would a Wooing Go." An illustration of this design was found in P.G. Konody's book, *The Art of Walter Crane.** Of the nine design blocks, only a portion of one was missing from our fragment. The paper was originally manufactured by Messrs. Jeffrey & Co. of London. A letter from Messrs. Arthur Sanderson & Sons Ltd., who took over from Jeffrey, reported the unhappy news that the "rollers" for the "Nursery Rhymes" paper had been destroyed. Although *The Art of Walter Crane* had a print of the entire paper a continued search was made for another fragment so that the missing piece might be copied exactly. Mrs. Frangiamore located more of the paper in the bathroom of the Visiting Nurses Association in Utica, New York. There, behind the wainscoting in the bathroom, which had been added around 1900, was the nursery paper. Several repeats were removed and added to the Memorial's collection. At last, with a complete document in hand, the paper could be reproduced. A wallpaper manufacturer agreed to undertake the exact reproduction of this paper, "Ye Frog He Would A Wooing Go."

The first step in the reproduction of any paper is to have the firm copy the art work exactly, so that it will be possible to use this copy in creating the color separations and the acetates from which the actual screens are cut. It is necessary to allow the manufacturer direct access to the original, and sometimes even to send it to him.

*London: George Bell & Sons, 1902.

However, nothing should be sent without a return receipt requested, nor without a covering letter listing exactly what is in the package. If an original document, a wallpaper, is lost, for whatever reasons, the restoration cannot proceed on the same ground as when the original was in existence.

In the case of the Nursery paper, the manufacturer required the original so he could verify the design and the colors in preparing the art work. It was sent to him by United Parcel Service, return receipt requested, with a letter listing the contents. Under separate cover he was sent a similar letter also listing the contents of the UPS shipment. A week later the firm called requesting the sample. The Memorial office had the receipt card and knew the parcel with the sample had been delivered and received. Everything was halted until the shipment was located (which it was) still in the packing carton in the back of a storeroom.

It is important to check carefully and to correct all the proofs for the reproduced wallpaper. Any errors made in the proofs will, of course, appear in the finished reproduction, unless caught and corrected.

When the acetates arrived it was dismaying to see that when the acetates were laid over the fragment the two did not match. Someone had altered the scale approximately 1/8 of an inch. Manufacturers who are willing to undertake reproductions often look at the design in terms of today's market. As one stated, "We did change the repeat, but you wouldn't want us to make the same mistakes that they made one hundred years ago, would you?" In a restoration one does not have that option. The satisfaction which comes from an exact copy more than outweighs the advantages of short cuts. The other reason for the change in scale was to be able to get two impressions from one screen, and save on the labor costs. The acetates were returned and had to be completely redone. Time is always a factor, but it is better to delay the schedule than to accept less than exact work.

Before the full production of the paper could proceed, the Memorial required a full color proof. When it arrived it was glorious. The animals matched, in form, in scale and were in order with the original, but the stock was the wrong color. Without the proper stock color it was useless to proceed further. After several at-

tempts, the firm secured the proper stock color, but then two of the
five colors used for the figures were wrong. After several additional
proofs, all was correct and the paper arrived.

Preliminary on-site research revealed the original ceiling designs.

The time to reproduce this wallpaper — two years — will appear to many to be a very long time. It might have been substantially less if the Memorial had not been so particular. When presenting an historic house or any restoration, the time required to achieve a quality product is well spent.

The ceiling of the Nursery was more difficult. The stenciled patterns survived in outline but there was no evidence of the colors. All the color had been washed off by later decorators. To solve this problem, the Restoration Committee elected to use the colors in the Walter Crane wallpaper in reproducing the ceiling pattern.

Today, as before, the Nursery looks as Clara Clemens remembered it. There is one detail that appears "strange" to modern parents. In the middle of the Nursery fireplace mantel is a J. & J. G. Lowe art tile of children dragging a dead bird, possibly a loose interpretation of Cock Robin's funeral. Appropriate to the Nursery? Well, the Clemenses thought so, for the tile was dated, and part of the original mantel. One must also remember that it was the age of "Struwelpeter" and Grimm's fairy tales, an age when children reveled in the lugubrious with childish fantasy and delight.

16

Susy's Room

Susy Clemens was the eldest and the favorite daughter of the family. Her room, adjoining the Nursery on one side and the second floor hall on the other, was described by Clara as "the little blue room" with a bed, high wardrobe, tables and chairs.[1] In scraping through the layers of paint no less than four wallpapers were found. Some of them overlapped, some did not. None of them were blue and all of the papers were of a palette more appropriate to the twentieth century than the nineteenth. In one corner of the room the investigation continued, and under the last layer of paint and paper there appeared to be only bare plaster. Under bright lights something else was detected. Faintly, ever so faintly, a design was visible, a design of little flowers, not of the Martha Washington variety, but more of the Eastlake variety, multi-pointed and scattered close together. Reference books showed similar patterns on walls, but no wallpaper books revealed anything close to the design. By careful measuring, and using the skills of master painters Leo and Bernie Sans, it was determined that this was not a stencil, not a wallpaper print, but a roller stencil design. That accounted for the closeness of the flowers and the short repeat. As the design was barely visible it was difficult to trace the faded and imprecise images. Frank Beaudin photographed the designs and the prints were blown up to full size. This made it possible to trace one or two of the groups of flowers, and finally to construct a full scale drawing. This drawing was taken to a local stamp works where rubber pads of the flowers were cast. When the pads were affixed to the roller, it was found that the impression was too shallow to leave a sharp, clean image. The flowers were then cut out, one by one, from the pad, and, in exact pattern, affixed to the roller. With a satisfactory pattern established, the debate began as to color. Clara had described the room as blue, and so a soft grey was chosen for the background, and the flower

*The delicate flower design created by the roller stencil was faintly
seen on the walls.*

pattern was roller-stenciled in blue. The effect is warm and
feminine.

Since Susy was the eldest, and since the Nursery reflected her
younger sisters, it was decided to decorate the room as Susy might
have had it when she was in her teens. Research provided that Susy
had bits of dried seaweed on her dressing table mirror. There was
also a letter from Mark Twain in 1885 advising Susy to decorate her
room as Julia Nast had: "All over the four walls could be seen
Christmas cards, menues, fans, statuettes, trinkettes with all im-
aginable dainty and pretty things massed upon them and hanging
from them—the most astounding variety of inexpensive and interesting trifles that was ever huddled together."[2] What makes this
room a special delight is that the walls are upholstered with dried
seaweed, fans, cards, photographs, posters and memorabilia.

17

Billiard Room

"Where do I write? In the billiard room, the very most satisfactory study that ever was. Open fire, register, and plenty of light."[1] Thus, Samuel L. Clemens described his billiard room, his study, his quiet zone. Located on the third floor, it was removed from the family and from the hustle and bustle of the Hartford house.

This room became a playroom and schoolroom for the Bissell children and their playmates. Later, it was an apartment. In 1958 it became an exhibition area when the Memorial acquired Mark Twain's billiard table from the descendants of his biographer, Albert Bigelow Paine. It was a stark and windy place, the painted walls and the woodwork lightened only by the green felt of the table and miscellaneous furniture. The table had not been in the Hartford house, but was the table which Mrs. Henry Huddleston Rogers presented to Mark Twain later in New York. Somewhere, perhaps, the great Hartford billiard table survives, with its black and gold legs, or maybe it fell apart during Mark Twain's life, necessitating the special gift from Mrs. Rogers.

Restoration of the Billiard Room began in 1962 with a grant from the Coe Foundation, in memory of Mai Rogers Coe, daughter of Henry H. Rogers. She was also a close friend of Mark Twain and a member of his exclusive Angel Fish Club.

Beneath one of the wooden moldings, samples of a rich red wallpaper and a dark floral paper were discovered. Both papers appeared to be pre-1900. The red paper occurred over the floral paper. But taking into consideration contemporary accounts of the room, and because Mark Twain used red in later billiard rooms, the Coe grant was used to reproduce the red paper and to clean the woodwork of its many layers of paint down to its original clear finish.

The ceiling proved to be a most perplexing and frustrating

The original Mahogany tiles that survived beneath layers of paint.

The Master Bedroom with the great Venetian bed.

The Schoolroom restored.

The original Nursery wallpaper was discovered beneath the mantel.

The Nursery restored.

Susy's room restored.

The Billiard Room restored.

Mark Twain by J. Carroll Beckwith. Painted at Onteora, N.Y., 1890.

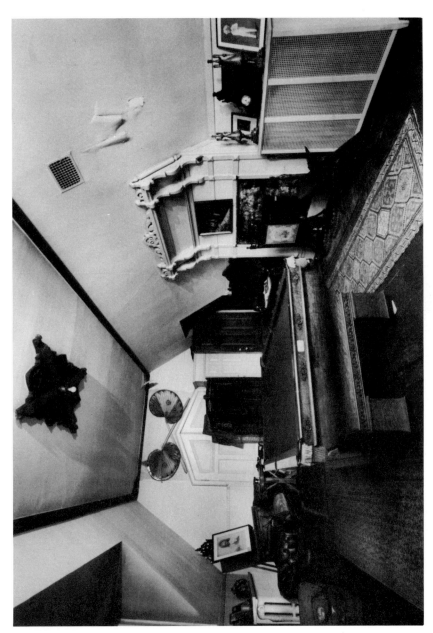

The Billiard Room when it was first opened as an exhibition area in the late 1950's.

project. It was covered by canvas which it was possible to document
as post-Clemens. The canvas was then numbered and removed.

A note should be added here on how stenciled designs were applied to walls and ceiling. In some cases, as with Associated Artists,
metallic paints were used. These tended to be of a very high quality
and very durable. More often than not, though, they used a
calcimine paint, which is water soluble, with the stenciled decorations painted in milk based pigments. Usually, when the Victorian
decorations became passé, the walls and ceilings were washed
down, and then repainted, or, due to cracks in the old plaster,
covered with canvas.

After documenting that a canvas is "late," it should be
numbered to preserve the sequence and removed very carefully. On
the backs of the canvas very often in the voids of the paste, the stenciled decorations are preserved. The paste apparently avoids the
milk based surfaces which acts as a "resist" and in so doing preserves
the pattern. Once given the key to a design, it is often possible to
return to the wall or ceiling in question and locate that design in the
wall or ceiling.

Hardly visible in the plaster of the Billiard Room ceiling were
crossed cues, "barrels of cigars," pipes and billiard balls. Was that
all? Ultraviolet photography revealed nothing. On the back of the
canvas, these designs, as well as stretcher borders of a geometric
design, were clearly seen. Closer inspection of the ceiling verified
the pattern. The design was not Tiffany, and, in 1977 it still was not
known who did the work.

Mrs. Shirley DeVoe of Bridgewater constructed full-scale cartoons of the designs. Because a trace of Eastlake red survived under
the center rosette, an Eastlake color scheme was adopted. Until
period photographs of this room are found it will not be known if
this pattern is exact. The pattern is in harmony with the room and
the elements which have been reproduced are fully documentable.
The design holds the ceiling and does not appear to be a restoration. The ceiling, what with debates and research, took some six
years to complete.

The last major element in the room, the fireplace, was not
completed until the fall of 1974. On the hearth were green floral
and red tiles. The bricks in the back had been severely altered to ac-

commodate a "modern" radiator, and all of the tiles in the surround had been destroyed. The back of the fireplace did not fit the opening and nothing made any sense, except for the pieces of the original woodwork which held the mantel shelf and ornamental carving. Other period fireplaces were looked at, other billiard rooms, anything which might furnish a clue to a solution. Finally, the Restoration Committee decided to proceed with the evidence at hand. Original woodwork which had been removed to accommodate the radiator was replaced. New brackets, matching others in the room, were carved to fit the holes in the mantel shelf and to support it. Kathryn Narrow, an artisan and instructor at the University of Hartford Art School, was enlisted to copy the hearth tile for use in the surround. When finished, the treatment blended with the rest of the room, and that, given very little evidence, is perhaps all one could ask.

On the back of the canvas the original stencil designs were preserved
in the voids of the paste.

The Bissells installed hardwood floors throughout the house but they did not bother to re-floor the Billiard Room. Instead, it had been painted over the years. The floor was carefully checked, using the same procedure that had been used on the walls. There were three early finishes on the floor, the first being a cinnamon stain, then a dark brown layer, and then a green layer. The floor was sanded down to the wood in two long swaths, revealing two continuous rows of tacks in a zigzag pattern. No tacks appeared around the perimeter of the room, but there was a 3/4 inch high molding strip, which ran along the bottom of the wood base.

Apparently the floor covering was held down by tacks in the center, and secured on the sides by the molding strip.

The next question was what type of covering was on the floor, if any? If rush matting had been used it would have left hundreds of tackholes and the floor bore no such marks. Strips of carpeting sewn into six-foot widths must have been used since 72-inch wide carpeting was not available. The carpets of the 1870's and 80's were manufactured in single widths of only 27 inches. The one exception was "ingrain" carpet which was manufactured in widths of thirty-six inches. The zigzag patterns of tacks would have held the two pieces of carpet together, and it would have been secured along the perimeter by the molding strip. From the attic of a cheese factory in North Colebrook, Connecticut, enough 1880 ingrain carpeting was secured to carpet the room.

It is still cold and windy in the Billiard Room on a March morning as it was when Howells wrote: "It was pretty cold up there in the early spring and late fall weather with which I chiefly associated the place, but by lighting up all the burners and kindling a reluctant fire in the hearth we could keep it well above freezing."[2]

Now, around the walls and on the shelves are mementos, a portrait of Prudence Crandall, Mark Twain's lithograph of "the Quaker City," his beer steins and clock, his billiard cue, and even his pencil sketch of a cow. Howells and others complained about the quantity of Scotch, the smoke from one of the interminable Twain cigars and the exhaustive conversation as well as his genuine passion for billiards. At the far end of the room are two marble windows. One has an "18" around the letter "C," the other a "74" around the letter "C." These were put in place by the author and his architect,

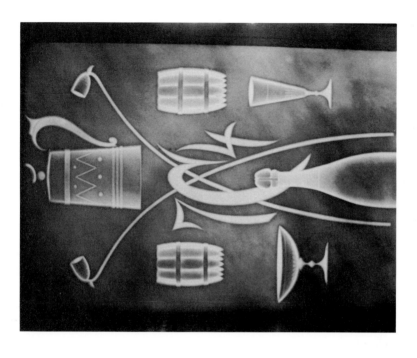

The two marble windows, created for Sam Clemens to celebrate the building of the house in 1874.

for this was Samuel L. Clemens' home, built in 1874. When these two marble windows first returned to the house they stood on the Library bookshelves awaiting some disposition. One day a researcher uncovered a contemporary account of Mark Twain's billiard room, specifically referring to these marble panels at the south end of the room. When taken upstairs they exactly fit the two spaces in the south wall.

It was his room, and around those figures are crossed cues, billiard balls, two long-stemmed pipes rampant, a beer stein, and a champagne glass, symbols of festivity and conviviality. These windows left the house in 1903 only to return and again to preside over that once so comfortable, sheltered existence.

18

Epilogue

When Mark Twain left the Hartford house, never to return, he eulogized it, and in those words expressed what he, his family and so many of the Victorian era felt about their homes. It is an understanding and a feeling which explains both the nature of the buildings and the character of the people who lived there.

> To us, our house was not unsentient matter—it had a heart, and a soul, and eyes to see us with; and approvals, and solicitudes, and deep sympathies; it was of us, and we were in its confidence, and lived in its grace and in the peace of its benediction.

> We never came home from an absence that its face did not light up and speak out its eloquent welcome—and we could not enter it unmoved.

If public symbols such as the Mark Twain house, were not available to visit and to study and to enjoy, our understanding and appreciation of the author and the period would be greatly foreshortened.

Visitors touring the house today are not aware of the restoration, are not aware of the trouble or the pain or the excitement which accompanied the renaissance of Mark Twain's house, and that is as it should be. This was the restoration of Mark Twain's house in Hartford, not the creation of a modern memorial to a committee or to prominent individuals. It is only when restorations appear to be merely great preservation projects that they have succeeded in their task.

The Costs of the Restoration

Chart of specific costs involved in the restoration of Mark Twain's house. The date indicates the year the cost was incurred, or the contracted estimate was made. Where specifically available a few miscellaneous items have been included, such as the cost of repairing and rewiring the gas fixtures in the Drawing Room.

DATE	AREA	PROJECT	COST
1960	Exterior	Roof	$27,500
1961	Exterior	Brick restoration	15,000
1966–1967	Front hall: Walls, ceiling, woodwork	Clean, canvas, decorate	13,500
1968–1969	Second floor hall Third floor hall Alcove	Canvas, decorate	14,000
1966–1968	Drawing Room: Walls, ceiling	Research, decorate	10,800
1972	Side brackets	Clean & repair, electrify	150
1973	Chandelier	Clean & repair, rewire	350
1972–1974	Ceiling, ceiling molding, mirror, rosette	Decorate, install, redecorate, install	5,700
1968	Dining Room:	Replace missing wood	1,300
1968	Woodwork	Stencil	2,000
1972	Walls, ceiling	Research, remove old paper, proposed ceiling designs	3,400

DATE	AREA	PROJECT	COST
1971	Dining Room: Wallpaper	100 rolls embossed paper	2,000
1972-1973	Wallpaper	Hand finish	9,500
1973	Dining Room Ceiling		5,500
1964	Library: Bookshelves	Woodwork	9,000
1970		Stretcher carving for bookshelves	3,500
1972		Corner brackets for bookshelves	2,000
1972	Cresting for mantel		250
1974	Overdoor carving		855
1968	Walls & ceiling	Research, replace ceiling, decorate	13,500
1972-1973	Miscellaneous	Brass plaque Lambrequins	2,000 300
1962-1963. 1973	Conservatory: Shade	Restoration	4,000 40
1971	Mahogany Guest Suite: Walls & ceiling	Research, removal of Potter sketch, replace ceiling, preparation of walls & ceiling	9,000
1972	Woodwork	Replace missing parts	750
1972	Wallpapers	Reproduction wallpaper (50 rolls for walls, 20 rolls for ceiling	3,500
1972	Wallpapers	Installation, painting	2,400
1974	Mark Twain's Bedroom: Walls, ceiling, woodwork	Research, remove old paper, canvas and decorate	13,500
1972	Schoolroom: Woodwork	Reproduce bench	750

DATE	AREA	PROJECT	COST
1972	Schoolroom:	Replace woodwork	1,700
1972	Walls & ceiling	Investigate & clean, prepare & decorate	11,500
1972–1973	Nursery: Fireplace	Masonry	650
1976	Walls & ceiling	Investigate, measure ceiling, prepare walls & ceiling, decorate ceiling	4,000
1972	Woodwork		1,500
1974	Wallpaper	Reproduce (44 rolls)	5,000
1974	Wallpaper	Hang	1,000
1972–1974	Susy's Bedroom: Walls & ceiling	Research, prepare designs, decorate ceiling	11,500
	Woodwork		2,000
1974	Wallpaper	Rubber stamps	150
1962	Billiard Room: Walls & ceiling	Check	2,000
1963	Wallpaper	Reproduce (40 rolls)	500
1964	Woodwork		200
1964	Woodwork Wallpaper	Clean Hang	2,000
1967	Ceiling	Investigate, proposed patterns, decorate	7,000
1968	Carpet	Clean & sew	325
1968	Lighting	Refinish fixture	50
1974	Fireplace	Woodwork, Tiles, Masonry	300 1,300 400

DATE	AREA	PROJECT	COST
	Miscellaneous		
1968	Halls & stairs	Carpeting	3,500
1973	Entire house	Window shades	600
1974	Drawing Room Dining Room Mahogany Room Library Mark Twain Bedroom Susy's Room Sitting Room (alcove) Schoolroom Nursery	Draperies, portieres, curtains	3,000

Footnotes

Preface
1. Wendell Garrett, *Antiques* (October, 1974) p. 627.

Chapter 4
1. Samuel L. Clemens, *Alta California* September 6, 1868.
2. Samuel L. Clemens, Samuel Charles Webster, ed. *Mark Twain, Business Man* (Boston: Little, Brown & Company, 1946) p. 123.
3. *The Hartford Daily Times*, March 23, 1874.
   William Dean Howells, *My Mark Twain* (New York: Harper & Brothers, 1910) p. 7.
4. (Samuel L. Clemens) Mark Twain. Dixon Wecter, ed. *The Love Letters of Mark Twain* (New York: Harper & Brothers, 1949) p. 326.

Chapter 5
1. Robert Koch, *Louis C. Tiffany, Rebel in Glass* (New York: Crown, 1964) p. 13.
2. Candace Wheeler, "The Philosophy of Beauty Applied to House Interiors," *Household Art* ed. Candace Wheeler (New York: Harper & Bros., 1893) p. 32.
3. Tiffany to Clemens, October 24, 1881. Mark Twain Papers, University of California at Berkeley. All material under copyright published by permission of Mr. Thomas Chamberlain and the Mark Twain Company, under the will of Clara Clemens Samassoud.

Chapter 6
1. (Samuel L. Clemens) Mark Twain, *Travelers Record*, January, 1877.
2. *The Hartford Daily Times*, March 23, 1874.

Chapter 7
1. Will M. Clemens, *Mark Twain His Life and Work: A Biographical Sketch* (San Francisco: Clemens Publishing Company, 1892) p. 167.
   Katherine S. Day, *Reminiscences,* 1930 Mark Twain Memorial Collection hereafter (MTMC).

2. George Parsons Lathrop, "A Model State Capitol" in Harpers New Monthly Magazine, October 1885, p. 731.
3. Will M. Clemens, *Mark Twain His Life and Work: A Biographical Sketch* (San Francisco: Clemens Publishing Company, 1892) p. 167.
4. Will M. Clemens, *Mark Twain His Life and Work: A Biographical Sketch* (San Francisco: Clemens Publishing Company, 1892) p. 167.

Chapter 8
1. Harriet Foote (Mrs. Herbert A.) Taylor to Edith Colgate Salsbury, May 5, 1959 (MTMC).
2. Candace Wheeler, "Philosophy of Beauty," p. 32.
3. Olivia Langdon (Mrs. Samuel L.) Clemens to Mr. Franklin G. Whitmore, May 2, 1903 (MTMC).
4. Clara Clemens to Robert H. Schutz, February 21, 1959 (MTMC).
5. Clarence Cook "What Should We Do With Our Walls?" (New York: Warren Fuller & Company, 1882) p. 30.

Chapter 9
1. Albert Bigelow Paine, *Mark Twain A Biography* (New York: Harper & Brothers, 1912) Vol. II, p. 661.
2. Katharine S. Day, *Reminiscences,* 1930 (MTMC).
3. Candace Wheeler, "The Philosophy of Beauty," p. 24.
4. Louis C. Tiffany to Mark Twain, November 17, 1881, Mark Twain Papers, Berkeley, California. All material under copyright published by permission of Mr. Thomas Chamberlain and the Mark Twain Company, under the will of Clara Clemens Samassoud.

Chapter 10
1. Jervis Langdon, *Samuel Langhorne Clemens* (privately printed) p. 14 (MTMC).
2. Lily Gillette Foote, *The Hartford Courant* September 23, 1885.
3. *Mark Twain's Notebook* (New York: Harper & Brothers, 1935) p. 212.
4. Mark Twain, *Tom Sawyer Abroad* (New York: Harper & Brothers, 1899) p. 426.
5. Edith Colgate Salsbury, *Susy and Mark Twain* (New York: Harper & Row, 1965) p. 223.

Chapter 11
1. William Dean Howells, *My Mark Twain* (New York: Harper & Brothers, 1910) p. 37.
2. Mary W. Edwards "Replanting of the Conservatory in Mark Twain's House in Hartford," March 1970 (MTMC).

Chapter 12
1. Mark Twain–Howells Letters Vol I, p. 129.
   Clara Clemens, *My Father Mark Twain* (New York: Harper & Brothers, 1931) p. 35.
2. William Dean Howells, *My Mark Twain* (New York: Harper & Brothers, 1910) p. 7.
3. Mary Lawton, *A Lifetime with Mark Twain* (New York: Harcourt Brace & Company, 1925) p. 131.
4. Clara Clemens to Margaret Graves, interview 1958 (MTMC).

Chapter 13
1. Clara Clemens to Robert H. Schutz, February 21, 1959 (MTMC).

Chapter 14
1. Clara Clemens, *My Father Mark Twain* (New York: Harper & Brothers, 1931) p. 88.

Chapter 15
1. Clara Clemens, *My Father Mark Twain* (New York: Harper & Brothers, 1931) p. 40.

Chapter 16
1. Clara Clemens, *My Father Mark Twain,* p. 40.
   Clara Clemens, Notations on the floor plans of the Mark Twain Memorial, (MTMC).
2. Edith Colgate Salsbury, *Susy and Mark Twain* p. 185.

Chapter 17
1. (Samuel L. Clemens) Mark Twain, Dixon Wecter, ed. *Mark Twain to Mrs. Fairbanks* (San Marino, Huntington, 1949) p. 205.
2. William Dean Howells, *My Mark Twain,* p. 14-15.

Chapter 18
1. (Samuel L. Clemens) Mark Twain, Albert Bigelow Paine, ed., *Mark Twain's Letters* (New York: Harper and Brothers, 1917) Vol II, p. 641.

Bibliography

Mrs. Thomas Bailey Aldrich. *Crowding Memories.* Boston: Houghton Mifflin Co., 1920.

Helen Post Chapman. *My Hartford of the Nineteenth Century.* Hartford: Edward Valentine Mitchell, 1928.

Clara Clemens. *My Father Mark Twain.* New York: Harper & Brothers, 1931.

(Samuel L. Clemens) Mark Twain. *Mark Twain's Autobiography:* With an introduction by Albert Bigelow Paine. Two Volumes. New York: Harper & Brothers, 1924.

_____. Samuel Charles Webster, ed. *Mark Twain Business Man.* Boston: Little, Brown & Company, 1946.

_____. *Mark Twain's Letters: Arranged with Comment by Albert Bigelow Paine.* Two volumes. New York: Harper & Brothers, 1917.

_____. Dixon Wecter, ed. *The Love Letters of Mark Twain.* New York: Harper & Brothers, 1949.

_____. *Mark Twain's Notebook: Prepared for Publication with Comments by Albert Bigelow Paine.* New York: Harper & Brothers, 1935.

_____. Dixon Wecter, ed. *Mark Twain to Mrs. Fairbanks.* San Marino, California: Huntington Library, 1949.

_____. *Tom Sawyer Abroad.* New York: Harper & Brothers, 1899.

_____. "This is the House that Mark Built," Travelers Record, January 1877.

_____, **and William Dean Howells.** Henry Nash Smith and William M. Gibson with the assistance of Frederick Anderson, eds. *Mark Twain—Howells Letters: The Correspondence of Samuel L. Clemens and William Dean Howells, 1872–1910.* Two Volumes. Cambridge: Belknap Press, 1960.

Will M. Clemens. *Mark Twain His Life and Work:* A Biographical Sketch. San Francisco: Clemens Publishing Company, 1892.

Clarence Cook. *"What Shall We Do With Our Walls?"* New York: Warren, Fuller & Co. 1882.

Henry Darbee, ed. *Mark Twain in Hartford.* Hartford: Mark Twain Memorial, 1958.

Wendell Garrett. The Magazine Antiques. New York, October 1974.

William Dean Howells. *My Mark Twain.* New York: Harper & Brothers, 1910.

Robert Koch. *Louis C. Tiffany, Rebel in Glass.* New York: Crown, 1964.

Mary Lawton. *A Lifetime with Mark Twain: The Memories of Katy Leary for Thirty Years His Faithful and Devoted Servant.* New York: Harcourt Brace & Co., 1925.

Jervis Langdon. *Samuel L. Clemens.* Privately Printed.

George Parsons Lathrop. "A Model State Capitol" Harper's Magazine, October 1885.

Albert Bigelow Paine. *Mark Twain, A Biography.* New York: Harper & Brothers, 1912.

Edith Colgate Salsbury. *Susy and Mark Twain.* New York: Harper & Row, 1965.

Candace Wheeler, "The Philosophy of Beauty Applied to House Interiors," *Household Art*, ed. by Candace Wheeler. New York: Harper & Brothers, 1893.

_____. *Yesterdays in a Busy Life.* New York: Harper & Brothers, 1918.